THE BRITISH FILM COLLECTION 1896-1984

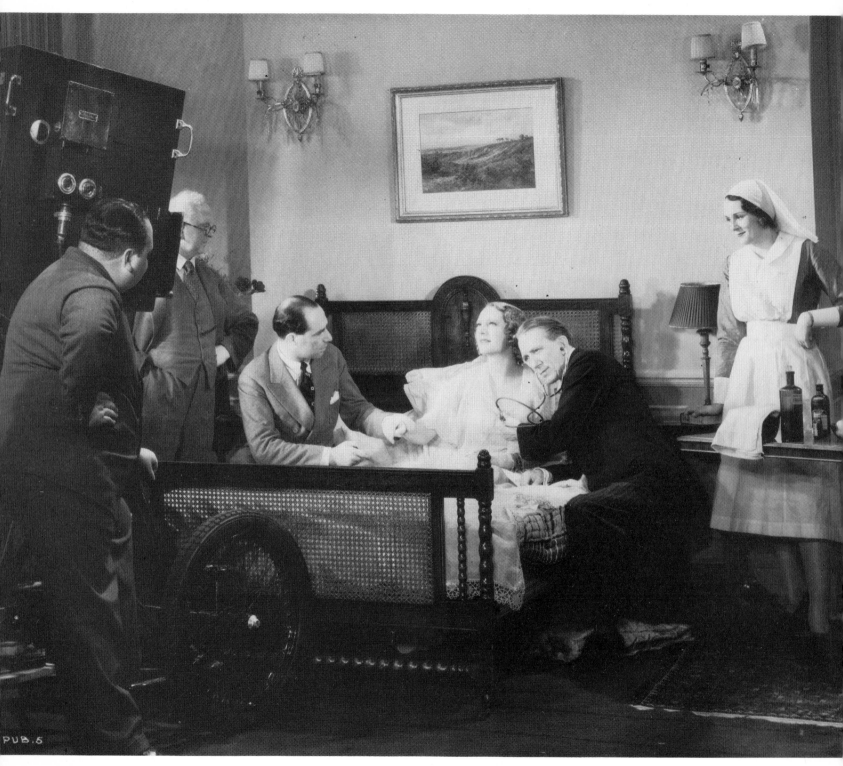

PUB.6

Alfred Hitchcock watching a scene from *Lord Camber's Ladies*
(BIP 1932), produced by Hitchcock and directed by Benn W.
Levy. Gertrude Lawrence appears happy with doctor Gerald du
Maurier, while nurse Benita Hume looks on.

THE BRITISH FILM COLLECTION 1896-1984

A History of the British Cinema in Pictures

PATRICIA WARREN

foreword by
SIR RICHARD ATTENBOROUGH

SALEM HOUSE
Salem, New Hampshire

This book is dedicated to the people and industry who were and are, The British Film Collection, *with affection and gratitude.*

First published in the United States
by Salem House, 1984. A member of
the Merrimack Publishers' Circle,
47 Pelham Road, Salem NH 03079

Copyright © 1984 by Patricia Warren

Book design by Norman Reynolds
Stills research by Patricia Warren
Research co-ordination by Andrew Warren

ISBN 0-88162-071-8
Library of Congress Catalog Card No: 84—051775

Printed and bound in Great Britain

Contents

Brighton Rock will long be remembered for Richard Attenborough's chilling portrayal of the razor-happy, baby-faced thug Pinkie Brown. (L. to r.) William Hartnell, Richard Attenborough and Harry Ross in a scene from the Boulting Brothers' production for ABPC in 1947. Hermione Baddeley, Carol Marsh and Nigel Stock also appeared.

Foreword

FUNDAMENTALLY, the medium of cinema is made up of individual frozen images, sometimes numbering hundreds of thousands, which, projected at precisely twenty-four frames per second, appear to move as smoothly as in real live action.

The early stills photographers, with their cumbersome *Speed Graphics* and heavy full plate negatives, worked mainly for the continuity and art departments. Their most important function was to record vital details of sets, props, costumes, together, of course, with the action of the artists. But, gradually, exhibitors began to demand photographs that they could display in glass fronted boxes outside the local *Odeon, Regal* or *Essoldo*. It was realised that glossy, high quality pictures, by giving a foretaste of the programme to be seen, drew audiences into the cinema.

And so stillsmen became an essential element in publicising and marketing films.

Cameras grew smaller, the half plate replacing the full. With the burgeoning of a star system, scene stills were no longer the only requirement. Portraits were needed that would depict screen idols in an idealised manner for their fans. The stills photographer had to learn lighting techniques to flatter faces that were perhaps less than perfect.

In the laboratories, where his work was processed and printed, he was backed up by retouchers, usually young women with endless patience and steady hands, whose job it was to eradicate every unsightly wrinkle and bestow upon each sitter an impossibly perfect complexion.

From half plate, stillsmen moved on to use the *Rollieflex* and negative became even smaller at two and a half inches square. Although much quieter in operation than the plate cameras had been, these were also too noisy to permit photography during actual shooting. But, by now, so important had still photographs become in selling a film that time was specially set aside for them to be taken.

At the beginning of the 50s, there came a revolution in technique. *Paris Match*, the French news magazine, was printing photographs from 35mm film — not always pinsharp but infinitely exciting because they conveyed movement, action, life.

Soon movie-stills cameramen, too, had changed over to the faster, smaller format film, many retaining the two and a quarter inch only for portraiture with the *Hasselblad*. However, in the 60s, when the star system began to be phased out, so too did the need for negatives of a size that could be retouched. No one wanted smooth, unreal faces any more. Kitchen sink, warts and all, was the order of the day.

With the triumph of reality over the air-brush, stills photography on the film set began to be recognised as an art form in itself.

The single picture, that frozen moment — be it in monochrome or in colour — should not merely itemise one instant in a completed movie. The stillsman's craft is to encapsulate the *essence* of an entire sequence, the *distillation* of an actor or actress's character.

Today, to do this, the unit photographer uses a battery of increasingly complex equipment; small, lightweight cameras that can be motorised at will, blimps that allow him to shoot without making a sound, a vast range of lenses, fine grain, high speed stock . . .

It is due to the diligence of Patricia Warren that this book charts not only the progress of stills photography in British films from 1896 to 1984, but, uniquely, in so doing records the history of the British film industry itself. For only in a work of this nature, so long overdue, can we take the time to examine in detail images that, in the cinema, are gone in less time than it takes to register their individuality.

Our thanks are due to Mrs Warren for saving so many stills from extinction and for selecting from her extraordinary archive a thousand of them, many never before published, which convey more than many millions of words.

It is indeed appropriate that this handsome and invaluable collection should appear in time to coincide with British Film Year; a celebration of indigenous talent both past and present, like this book, but also heralding the bright future that lies ahead.

Richard Attenborough
1984

Introduction
& Acknowledgments

THE SUCCESS of my first book, *Elstree: The British Hollywood*, was due in no small measure to the stills and photographs researched from the Thorn EMI Elstree Studios, and from industry and private sources. The history of the British Cinema is essentially a visual one and an in-depth British Film Collection seemed long overdue. I am again fortunate in being able to include an amount of hitherto unpublished photographs as well as many old favourites.

Confronted with such a vast subject and thousands of stills — although the producers and directors are given for each film still shown — the emphasis in this instance is placed on the stars, much loved character actors and comedians, landmark and small budget films and atmosphere of each decade. Producers, directors, technicians and studios, will have another book dedicated to them in the future, although I hope that they will not feel neglected in this one. Film dates given are in the main related to their initial exhibition.

It is important to me that *The British Film Collection* should entertain as the film industry has done over the decades, as well as being a source of reference for the industry, film student and film buff alike. Because of the sheer enormity of the subject, there will inevitably be a sense of disappointment, if the book should not include a favourite film or star. For any such omissions, I apologise in advance, with a promise to make amends in the future, but hope that in any case the book will bring back many happy memories — if perhaps a few sad ones.

Some of the best and worst British characteristics are reserve and self-effacement, and we often destroy our labours of love, in other people's eyes, when we self-indulgently denigrate the results of our efforts: sometimes without analysing the merits of the individual ingredients that went into their making. With uncharacteristic pride then, I give you *The British Film Collection*, not because I have written the book, but because of the people and industry, who made it possible.

*   *   *

Film buffs will note an amount of hitherto unpublished still material and my special thanks and appreciation go to the following people who have not only provided stills and archive material but also for their unstinting help and support. Every effort has been made to trace the copyright holders of the photographs and quoted material. Should there be any omissions in this respect, we apologise and shall be pleased to make the appropriate acknowledgement in future editions: Tim Angel, B.A.F.T.A., Beaver Films Ltd., Monty Berman, Brent Walker, Black Lion Films, Children's Film and Television Foundation, Columbia Picture Corp., Walt Disney Productions, Dovemead Ltd., Dresser Films Ltd., Eon Productions Ltd., Euston Films, G.W. Films Ltd., Gala Film Distributors, Goldcrest Films, Golden Communications, Handmade Films, Marcel Hellman, Cyril Howard, Hugh Hudson, Indo British Films Ltd., I.T.C. Entertainment, Bryan Langley, Robert Lennard, Euan Lloyd, London Film Productions, Stuart Lyons, Kenneth Maidment, Eric Maxwell, Merchant Ivory Productions, MGM/UA Pictures, Andrew Mitchell, National Film and Television School, Peter Noble, Dame Anna Neagle, Paramount, Alan Parker, PIC Publicity, David Puttnam, Punch, Rank Film Distributors, Geoff Reeve Films, R.K.O., Romulus Films Ltd., David Samuelson, Sam Spiegel, Thorn EMI Films Ltd., Twentieth Century-Fox Film Co., Vic Films, Warner Bros., David Wickes, Sir John Woolf, Universal. Cartoons are by courtesy of Punch.

My profound gratitude also goes to Sid Clements and the Rank, Pinewood Studios stills department, Jack Middleton and the Thorn EMI Elstree Studios stills department, Michelle Snapes and the B.F.I. stills department and the staffs of Richmond and Twickenham Public Libraries. Last but by no means least a very special thank you to my husband Andrew Warren, who co-ordinated the mammoth amount of research material and also supplied additional research and to Elm Tree Books, who gave splendid help and support throughout the project.

CHAPTER ONE

How it all began

1896-1909

WHAT SORT of people, one might ask, would have been attracted to this new development of movement on film in the last years of the nineteenth century? Were they all Cecil B. de Milles in the making? A great many of them, such as William Friese-Greene, who built the first practical movie camera in 1889, were inventors, photographers and chemists whose fathers had entertained the family and friends on Saturday evenings with a magic lantern show — an early form of projector which threw an enlarged image of a transparency on to a white sheet or tablecloth — and whose homes were adorned with genteel portraits of the family (all looking as if they were about to meet the firing squad) from the local photographer.

The first major British film pioneers were William Friese-Greene, Birt Acres, R. W. Paul, Esme Collings, G. A. Smith, Cecil Hepworth, James Williamson, Will Barker, Walter Haggar and Walter D. Welford. Drawing on their home background, education and visionary perception — either academic or artistic — they and their pupils effectively founded the British film industry from 1896 to the turn of the century.

Although several of them would have been horrified at the thought of their scholarly achievements being paraded as fairground attractions — which for a time they were — in the main, there was a natural progression from the filming of moving objects such as horse-drawn buses and people, to local events, then news items and finally the true start of feature production, the filming of simple stories.

These first offerings in 1896 consisted of 40 feet of film projected at an average speed of one foot per second — not very lengthy by any standards. By 1900 some had progressed to 200 feet, although the average film was under 100 feet.

Amongst the productions of 1896 were *The Boxing Kangaroo*, a boxing bout between a man and a kangaroo, and *Tom Merry, Lightning Cartoonist* from Birt Acres; *The Soldier's Courtship* and *Mr Maskelyne Spinning Plates and Basins*, a conjuring act from R. W. Paul; and *The Broken Melody*, a romantic melodrama from Esme Collings.

In 1897 G. A. Smith entered the arena with his comedy *Nursing the Baby* and *Making Sausages*, while Walter D. Welford showed *Repairing a Puncture* in all of 40 seconds! Quick to realise the advertising potential, Nestlés and Lever Brothers in a joint promotional exercise made one of the first British commercials, *The Sunlight Soap Washing Competition*, which was supplied free when other films were booked from the film agencies. By 1898 Cecil Hepworth had also started producing his own films which included *Exchange Is No Robbery*, a 50-foot comedy. James Williamson provided excellent competition with his own humorous sketches like *The Jealous Painter*, in which the hero poured whitewash over his rival and *Norah Mayer The Quick Change Dancer*, advertised as 'eccentric dances'.

By the turn of the century the Warwick Trading Company, headed by American Charles Urban was well into production, and William George Barker and Walter Haggar were to follow. Hot on their heels came Bamforth and Company who teamed up with the Riley Brothers of Bradford, Randall Williams, Mitchell and Kenyon, Cricks and Sharp, the Clarendon Film Company and the Sheffield Photo Company. They were now joined by the British Mutoscope and Biograph Company, which started as a branch of an American company, and the French Gaumont company whose British branch had been inaugurated by A. C. Bromhead and T. A. Welsh in 1898.

In the early days of film production, daylight, though not always on its best behaviour, was sufficient to capture the filming of simple movement in local events or news items. As story lines came into being, the proud pioneer inveigled his family into performing the roles and assisting with any necessary 'props', while his garden or local park provided adequate setting. But as it became clear that there was a definite commercial outlet for these productions and the stories became more sophisticated, then production techniques followed suit. By today's standards they would be considered crude in the extreme, though many of the basic principles are still followed.

It became necessary, for example, for interiors to be shown, rather than making do with the heroine pointing vaguely in the direction of a house, while costumes, scenery and, above all, lighting became essential commodities. Budgets had now to be considered, and if the light failed, then the filming had to stop. So studios were beginning to be built, not by any means the elaborate structures of later years, but simple wooden stages, usually in the open air.

GREAT SCOTT!
THEY MUST BE SHOWING A
HEPWORTH FILM

Former arc lamp designer Cecil Hepworth, son of a famous lantern lecturer, had toured the country with his own cinematograph show, before setting up a film-printing laboratory and production company at Walton-on-Thames. His first stage, in the back garden of his Walton home, measured 10ft by 6ft and the scenery was painted in the kitchen. The Sheffield Photo Company were somewhat more affluent, their open-air stage being 20ft long by 9ft wide. The only drawback was a doorway and a window on the back wall which had to be papered over for every new scene; sadly, daylight was often fading by the time the papering was finished. Former amateur photographer Will Barker was certainly courageous with his open-air studio at Stamford Hill — a stage, two scaffolding rods and a backcloth — and although these humble beginnings turned in quick profits, it was slowly becoming apparent to everyone that these were not ideal working conditions. Of the Brighton school, one-time portrait photographer G. A. Smith and former chemist James Williamson went in for glasshouses for maximum sunlight, while R. W. Paul's famous studio at New Southgate — no doubt reflecting his former occupation as a scientific instrument-maker — went in for glass and gadgetry. Well ahead of its time, it sported a trolley mounted on rails that carried the camera, a scenery-painting room, special trap-doors and a hanging frame at the back of the stage on which backcloths could be fixed. Perhaps the most innovative studio in the country was that of the Mutoscope and Biograph Company behind the Tivoli in the Strand which had a revolving studio, able to turn in the direction of the best light. Undeterred, the film-makers pressed on. By this time, the excitement and promise of this mushrooming industry was gaining momentum and investment at an incredible rate. The Clarendon Film Company bought studio premises at Croydon, and Cricks and Sharp purchased a property at Mitcham, consisting of a cottage which they used for an office and laboratory — and a greenhouse which served as studio and laboratory.

Meanwhile, the intimate Saturday evening parlour sessions with Father's magic lantern had given way to more sophisticated methods of film exhibition. By the turn of the century, films were a popular attraction at civic centres, variety halls and fairgrounds. Indeed the British Mutoscope and Biograph Company were making films not only for general exhibition, but also for their penny-in-the-slot machines which could be found in every respectable fairground. Variety theatres were making way for a 'moving picture' slot on their bill, while hall owners were beginning to consider if it might not be worth their while to put on a full-time film show, with a variety act in the interval.

This train of thought naturally led to the first system of distribution. Exhibitors started to become film renters and by the turn of the century, the competitive market had reduced the price of film from one shilling to eightpence per foot (5—3.3 new pence) which then became a standard sixpence (2.5p) per foot. By 1905/6, production companies like Cecil Hepworth and exhibitors like Walker and Turner were advertising films for hire and the market became confused. Not only were the producers selling on the open market, but exhibitors were also stock-piling, selling and hiring on the same level, which often meant that an identical film was for sale and for hire from two different sources at the same time. It was around this time that the concept of exclusive selling rights, rather than exclusive renting rights, entered the industry, and some producers started to use large film trading companies such as Gaumont and Charles Urban as their selling agents. It was however a far cry from the modern-day pattern of distribution.

Publicity was also beginning to play a vital role in advertising a film, though present day promotional copy would seem very tame against the text put out by one British distributor in 1902 for a film called *Fight With Sledgehammers*, which read as follows:

'Two blacksmiths bash each other to pulp with hammers, throw iron bars at each other, and all for the love of a girl. See the sensational ending in which Joe holds Fred's head on his anvil and is about to bang his brains out with a sledge hammer but is prevailed upon by the girl to spare the other's life. See the victor crawl battered and bleeding across the floor, his all but senseless form dragged up on to its feet by the policeman who takes him into custody.'

It is interesting to note that the heroic blacksmith was played by a Mr A. W. Fitzgerald, while the heroine was played by Mrs Fitzgerald. The fact that they managed to achieve all this in the space of two-and-a-half minutes should not be taken as a reflection on their marital relationship.

Although the industry was still in its infancy, a subtle change was also taking place with regard to casting. As professional exhibitions began to take root, it became increasingly clear to the producer that neither the renter nor the audiences were going to pay good money to see his wife and offspring playing charades up there on the ever expanding screen, particularly if his good lady was as plain as a pikestaff and little Flora had rickets. No, the time had come to engage professional actors and actresses who, while considering the film industry vulgar beyond belief (because of its fairground and variety hall associations), might be coaxed into a studio between shows if the remuneration was sufficiently generous. Of course if one was clever enough to discover one's own artists and build up a stock company, then so much the better. Producer Cecil Hepworth may have missed signing up Charlie Chaplin, who found fame and fortune in the States, but he did discover two local schoolgirls whom he cast in his famous *Tilly* series. Chrissie White and Alma Taylor became Britain's first film stars. Other producers took note and followed suit.

SMALL PICTURES: Amateur pioneer of the British film industry, R. W. Paul, was one of the first to show films commercially and actually charged an admission fee to one of the first 'Motion Pictures' performances shown at Olympia in March 1886. These pictures from his Muswell Hill Studios illustrated catalogue were designed, photographed and copyrighted by him in 1898 and entitled *Kitchen* and *Exhibition.*

BOTTOM RIGHT: Born in 1874, Cecil Hepworth was the son of a famous lantern lecturer, T. C. Hepworth and entered the film world by selling photographic equipment of his own design. In 1897 he wrote one of the earliest books on cinematography and a year later set up his own film laboratory at Walton-on-Thames. In 1899 he started to produce films and by the turn of the century the Hepworth Manufacturing Company was making approximately a hundred films a year; a figure that had already doubled by 1906.

TOP RIGHT: Cecil Hepworth filming the Derby from the top of a horse-drawn bus in 1899.

CENTRE RIGHT: Birt Acres filming the Derby in 1895.

BOTTOM: **Birt Acres in his photographic workshop** Many of the early British film inventors came into the world of cinematography through chemistry, photography or the optical lantern (known as the magic lantern, an early form of projector throwing an enlarged image of a transparency on to a white screen). Birt Acres had worked with R. W. Paul and his experimental work with the Kinetic Lantern and subsequent demonstration of projecting motion pictures before members of the Royal Photographic Society met with great success. In 1896 he founded the Northern Photographic Works Ltd., but unlike R. W. Paul, he preferred the academic approach to the cinematograph rather than the commercial one, probably viewing with horror the thought of his invention being exhibited as a music-hall turn.

ABOVE: **Will Barker**
William George Barker moved swiftly from being a 'free show' amateur producer, director, camera-man in 1896 to being a professional visionary. By 1901 he had founded the Autoscope Company and in the same year opened his open-air studio (a stage, two scaffolding rods and a back-cloth) at Stamford Hill. These humble beginnings turned in a quick profit and were superseded in 1904 by his studio at Ealing, a location that was to earn itself a very special place in the history of the British film industry. Barker became known for his lavish productions and eye for detail which belied his seemingly casual approach to casting. 'Can anyone swim?' he bellowed at an attentive crowd waiting outside his *Hamlet* production office. 'A little,' came a timid female response from the back. 'Good,' Barker replied, 'you can play Ophelia.'

TOP: **The Williamson Studios**
It was very common in the early days of film making to involve the entire family. In 1898, James Williamson decided to sell his chemist's shop in Hove and concentrate on the photographic side of that promising new industry — motion pictures. Aided and abetted by his loved ones, he proceeded to make family cast films in the garden of his new premises in Hove in which he often appeared and which he frequently wrote. He would then develop, print and sell his productions to early distributing companies like Butcher, Gaumont and Urban.

BOTTOM: Butcher catalogue of Williamson's films.

Walter Haggar

Flair, showmanship, family loyalty and free enterprise seemed the ideal formula for anyone venturing into the new film industry at the turn of the century. Purpose-built cinemas were yet to come, so venues would be fairgrounds, variety and church halls and in more than one case, abandoned chapels. Haggar was a larger-than-life travelling showman who, having acquired a camera made 'locals' of topical and scenic interest. He then turned his camera on to the fairground celebrities and events which, in turn, became comic scenes and stories. Again, in many cases, his family would be called in to support the current production, as actors, scene shifters, wardrobe mistresses etc. It also helped if someone could play the piano — music being an essential ingredient of silent film entertainment. For a man without a studio, Haggar's achievements for that period were quite phenomenal. Although his output was naturally less than that of his studio or house-based contemporaries, his films became extremely successful and he commenced story-line production on a grand scale. *The Salmon Poachers,* the *Mirthful Mary* series and his *Life of Charles Peace* were much sought after by other exhibitors and generally acclaimed as important film contributions to their era.

TOP: *A Desperate Poaching Affray*, directed by Walter Haggar in 1903.

BOTTOM: *Life of Charles Peace,* directed by William Haggar, 1905.

"HOPE SPRINGS ETERNAL."

THE CINEMA AS AN EDUCATIVE FORCE.

TOP LEFT AND RIGHT:
Early Trick Photography
Arthur Melbourne Cooper had made one of the earliest known British examples of animation (and probably commercials) when in 1899 he made a film for Bryant & May which in effect was an appeal for funds to supply the troops in South Africa — not for ammunition, food or clothing but . . . matches — something the Ministry seemed to have overlooked. Some years later, Mebourne Cooper made two delightful films, featuring animated toys, *The Tale of The Ark,* 1909 and *Dreams of Toyland,* 1908.

BOTTOM RIGHT: As producers slowly gained confidence in film making, taking on a variety of roles behind the camera, it was gradually beginning to dawn on variety and circus artists, as well as actors and actresses, that the artistic and earning potential on the other side of the lens was enormous. Amongst their ranks was one Charles Spencer Chaplin. Born in London 1889, he joined Fred Karno's pantomime at an early age and while on tour with them in America received an invitation to act in comedies for the Keystone Company. Charlie Chaplin became a legend within his own lifetime. His seal-like shuffle, baggy trousers, black bowler, moustache, cane and huge, soulful eyes made him a star, epitomising the silent screen for ever. He is seen here at 17 years of age (middle of bottom line).

TOP RIGHT: Charlie Chaplin as the world came to know him.

BELOW: Towards the end of the first decade of the 20th century, purpose-built cinemas were replacing the fairground and variety halls that had been the traditional venues for film exhibition. Up to this time, no serious theatrical artist would be seen dead on a film set — acting or otherwise, because of its music-hall and fairground origins. Hoping to cloak the industry with at least a superficial respectability, and with an eye to the cash-flow, film-makers started to lure famous thespians to their studios with promises of extravagant Shakespearian productions and fat remunerations. In 1913 Sir Johnston Forbes-Robertson was to make one of the most important British Shakespearian films of its time — his production of *Hamlet* for Hepworth under the auspices of The Gaumont Company.

MANNERS AND MODES.
HERO-WORSHIP: DISTRACTIONS OF THE FILM WORLD.

BOTTOM: Alma Taylor (l.) and Chrissie White. Two early British film stars of the silent screen who started their careers in 'shorts' whilst still schoolgirls and became famous in the *Tilly* series, shown here, produced by Cecil Hepworth at Walton-on-Thames.

Make and break

1910-1919

BY 1910, films had become the entertainment of the masses. Purpose-built picture theatres/cinemas had made their appearance in 1908 and by 1913 Greater London had 600 picture houses. The *Kinematograph Year Book* survey of 1914 showed a total of 925 theatres covering the large towns of Britain and 242 in the county towns.

In 1912, the British Board of Film Censors was set up to approve films for public viewing. The Cinematograph Act of 1909 had established the right of local authorities to ban films on grounds of impropriety; the variety of decisions taken across the country led to a chaotic situation and the film trade itself, led by the Cinematograph Exhibitors Association (formed in 1912), took steps to set up a central censoring body whose decisions should be valid throughout Britain. Of the 7488 films examined by the British Board of Film Censors in its first year of existence in 1913, exception was taken to 166 for reasons including indecorous dancing; situations accentuating delicate marital relations; indecorous sub-titles; and confinements. 22 films were rejected entirely on the following grounds: cruelty to animals; excessive drunkenness; holding up a Minister of Religion to ridicule; impropriety in conduct and dress; indecent dancing; indelicate accessories in the staging; indelicate or suggestive sexual situations; judicial executions; materialism of Christ or the Almighty; native customs in foreign lands abhorrent to British ideas; and subjects depicting procurations, abduction and seduction.

Meantime British studios had sprung up around the country and by 1911 were beginning to hold their own against American competition. They were not to know that World War I would practically annihilate their young industry. From 1906 to 1914 studios were located at Alexandra Palace, Bushey, Catford, Clapham, Croydon, Crystal Palace, Ealing, East Finchley, Elstree, Esher, Hackney, Hounslow, Isleworth, Kew Bridge, Leytonstone, Merton Park, New Southgate, Teddington, Thames Ditton, Twickenham, Victoria, Walthamstow, Walton-on-Thames, Wardour Street, Whetstone, St Albans and — the few outside the greater London area — at Bradford, Brighton, Hastings, Holmfirth and Manchester.

Although a number of pioneers were still running their own studios, like Williamson at Brighton and Hepworth at Walton-on-Thames, a number had already fallen by the wayside and new companies

and names were making their mark, if not always superb films. Sir Hubert von Herkomer, a Royal Academician, was anxious to participate in the creation of film as an art form. Having gained a little experience with Pathé, he built a studio in the garden of his Bushey home 'Lululand' and enthusiastically went into production with his son Siegfried. They turned out several 'lulus' before poor Sir Hubert died a year later. It should however be noted that the trade regarded him with some awe, doggedly lavishing praise on his work, and also that his studio at Bushey — along with those at Twickenham — is one of the oldest in the country.

The London Film Company, located in a former skating rink at Twickenham, was founded by Dr Ralph Jupp in 1913 and was the largest in the UK at the time. The Neptune Studios were opened at Elstree by former London Film Company employees, actor/manager John East and producer Percy Nash, a year later. Merton Park Studios, Shepherd's Bush Studios and the G. B. Samuelson Studios at Worton Hall, Isleworth all opened their doors in the first half of the decade. After the war had ended in 1918, the Welsh-Pearson Company founded studios at Craven Park, and the Stoll Film Company acquired the services of director Maurice Elvey, making their first film in a converted ballroom before going on to open their new studios at Cricklewood in 1919.

But what of the films and the stars between 1910 and 1920? Up to the outbreak of the war in 1914, a number of studios had indeed succeeded in developing their own stock players — stars from the stage, the beginning of the star system in fact. The Neptune Studios had their own stock company with Frank Tennant and Daisy Cordell, while Hepworth had made stars out of Chrissie White and Alma Taylor. The art of the silent film comedian was at its zenith and the Bamforth Company in Yorkshire made a star out of its comedian Reggie Switz in the famous *Winky* series — 39 films in all, with such titles as *Winky Accused of an 'Orrible Crime* and *Winky and the Cannibal Chief*, most of them running for about eight minutes. The public also flocked to see *Pimple*, as played by slapstick clown Fred Evans in a series of films. Some of the 130 titles were made at the Eel Pie Island studios at Twickenham. Then, of course, there was the brave Lieutenant Daring as played by Percy Moran and his successors in such offerings as *Lt. Daring Avenges an Insult to the Union Jack* and *Lt.*

Daring and the Photographing Pigeon. Meantime, Clarendon stars P. G. Norgate and Harry Lorraine portrayed Lt. Rose in an equally long series which included such epics as *Lt. Rose and the Sealed Orders* and *Lt. Rose and the Stolen Submarine.* Violet Hopson, Blanche Forsythe, Florence Turner, Ellaline Terriss, Dorothy Bellew and Jane Gail became popular stars, while Gerald Lawrence, Owen Nares, Harry Royston and Henry Ainley had their first taste of screen stardom.

The films themselves were numerous and varied, from Clarendon's *The Convent Gate,* Hepworth's *Wealthy Brother John, David Copperfield* and *Oliver Twist,* to Barker's famous *Jane Shore. Lady Windermere's Fan, The Vicar of Wakefield* and *East Lynne,* to name but a few, were very successful.

During the war years, propaganda films and stories of a patriotic nature — with titles like *For King and Country* and *A Patriotic English Girl* — became firm favourites. On the home commercial front, the Kinematograph Renters Society (now the Society of Film Distributors) was formed in 1915. The British film industry had developed so rapidly that before the outbreak of war it had become something of a threat to the American home market — a unique turnabout. This also meant, however, that the British were to find distribution outlets in the States extraordinarily difficult.

Nevertheless, the industry's fighting spirit could still be seen on the home front from at least one renter — International, whose monthly publicity brochure in 1916 carried such slogans as 'While always willing to speculate, are we likely to gamble with our reputation?', 'Are we likely to back a picture that won't succeed?' and 'We have complete confidence in our judgement and care nothing for outside opinions, the past is proof. . . .' Amongst their

offerings for 1916 was *The Man Who Bought London,* a five-reeler, produced by F. Martin Thornton for the Windsor Film Company and starring Mr Edward Arundell, Miss Evelyn Boucher and Mr Roy Travers.

By the end of the war in 1918, it was clear that Britain had lost much ground in film production. Many actors and technicians simply had not returned from the war, studios had deteriorated and America had regained its former dominant position. It was a case of starting from scratch all over again . . . provided that one had something to scratch with.

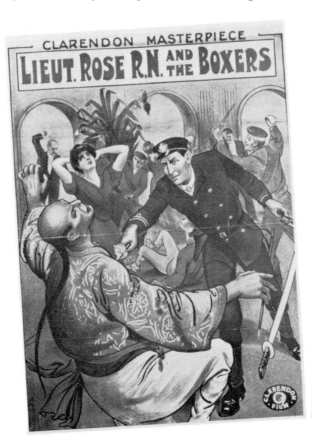

SMALL PICTURES:
Richard III
Luring famous stage actors to appear in the new silent motion pictures was one thing, but having acquired their services, how would one utilise them? The obvious answer was to transpose established stage productions directly on to the screen. Daring, but not always successful. Stage actors of the period — used to booming across the footlights without modern amplification — were horrified when confronted by a producer/director who did not require their finest assets, their voices. Emphasis was therefore placed on their facial and physical interpretation, which resulted in much overplaying. Traditional stage grouping and sets sometimes added to the impression that the spectator was watching a dumb, alcoholic cast through a misted window pane — from the front of the stalls. Here, Frank Benson as Richard III, woos the Lady Anne (Constance Benson, top left) and is roundly cursed (centre left). Other scenes show the murder of the Duke of Clarence. A two-reeler, it was produced by the F. R. Benson Company with the Stratford Memorial Production cast which included Violet Farebrother, Murray Carrington and Eric Maxon in 1911.

INSET: The Cricks & Martin production of *The Fairy Bottle*, directed by Dave Aylott, starring Una Tristam and Bill Hayley, 1913, and *The Reward of Perseverance*, a Barker production, directed by Bert Haldane in 1912.

BOTTOM: Chrissie White (l.) and Gladys Sylvani, both popular Hepworth stars, appeared in *Wealthy Brother John* in 1911, the tale of a rich man testing the motives of his family. Directed for Hepworth by Bert Haldane.

TOP: This still might look as if it belongs to *Lt. Daring RN and the Photographing Pigeon*, but in fact comes from *Through the Clouds*, produced by B. & C. and directed by Charles Weston in 1913. Harry Lorraine (r.) often played Lt. Daring whilst Ernest G. Batley (l.) made an enormous contribution to the silent era as actor, writer and director. Splattered George Foley — a silent star with over 60 films to his credit — also appeared in a number of Lt. Daring films as well as the *Walter* series.

BELOW: Film posters of 1912.

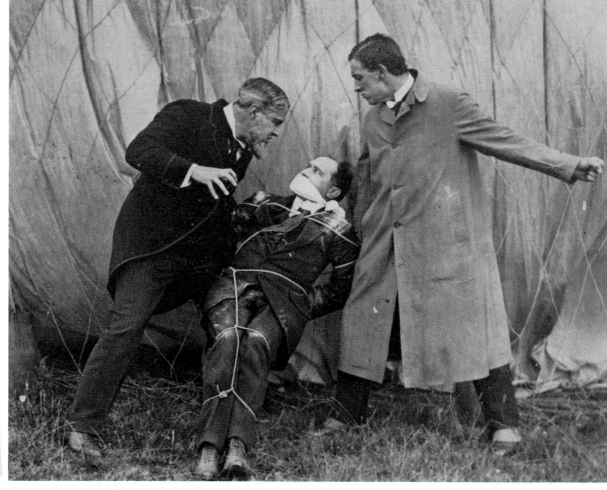

BOTTOM: The trend of adapting classic novels for the screen developed rapidly. Hepworth's *Oliver Twist*, directed by Thomas Bentley, was the first UK attempt to develop a complete volume in depth. Here Harry Royston as Sikes threatens an imploring Nancy, played by Alma Taylor, 1912.

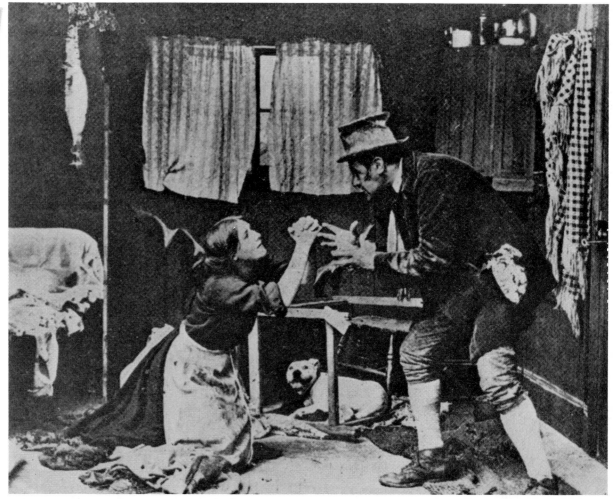

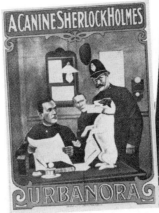

TOP LEFT: One of the earliest of screenwriters was the Marchioness of Townsend who wrote the script for the Clarendon production of *The Convent Gate*, directed by Wilfred Noy and starring Dorothy Bellew, 1913.

TOP CENTRE: *A Canine Sherlock Holmes*, starring Spot, the Urbanora Dog in 1912. Produced by the Urban Trading Company and directed by Stuart Kinder.

TOP RIGHT: *Allan Field's Warning.* A Barker production. This tale of a gambler turning to crime after a nightmare starred Fred Paul and Blanche Forsythe and was directed by Bert Haldane in 1913.

CENTRE RIGHT: Maurice Elvey and friends. Elvey made his directorial debut in 1913 with two films, *Maria Marten: A Murder in the Red Barn* and *The Great Gold Robbery*, both for the Motograph Film Company at their Crystal Palace Studios.

BOTTOM RIGHT: A 1913 poster for *Blood and Bosh*, directed by Hay Plumb for Hepworth.

BOTTOM LEFT: Miss Ellaline Terriss, a popular actress of the period who worked for the Zenith Film Company, formed to film popular stage productions at their Whetstone Studios.

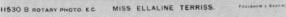

ABOVE: **Twickenham Film Studios**
In 1913 the London Film Company, founded by Dr Ralph Jupp, heralded their first release, *The House of Temperley* from their studios at Twickenham. Harold Shaw's production from the novel *Rodney Stone* by Conan Doyle met with great success. Formerly a skating rink, the studio was the largest in the UK at that time. Over 70 years on, the Twickenham Film Studios, headed by Guido Coen, still carry their proud tradition of British film-making into the future.

RIGHT: 'We have some good news, and some bad news . . .' Charles Hawtrey looks more than a little floored on seeing his Martian visitor in *Message From Mars,* a 1913 Nicholson Ormsby-Scott production. Directed by J. Wallett Walker.

TOP: A film poster of 1913.

BOTTOM LEFT: A proud moment for G. B. Samuelson (r.) at the opening of his English mansion, Worton Hall Studios, on the 1st July, 1914. Seen here with his brother Julian Wylie and Vesta Tilley who performed the opening ceremony. Born in 1887, George Berthold Samuelson spent his early business years as a film hirer in Birmingham, then having achieved success co-producing *Sixty Years a Queen* with Will Barker, he decided to form his own company, buy a studio and produce and direct his own films. The Samuelson Film Manufacturing Company was founded in 1914; 70 years on the Samuelson Film Service Ltd — an international organisation operated by his sons and grandchildren — is synonymous with film and television equipment and services throughout the world.

BOTTOM RIGHT: The Worton Hall Mansion Studio in 1914.

ABOVE: With the outbreak of war in 1914, the British film industry went into decline. Whilst almost a generation of British manhood was being devoured as gun fodder in the French trenches, British studio production was left to limp along as best as it could. Government-sponsored propaganda films such as *Women in Munitions* did much for morale, but little for entertainment on the home front. American products began to flood the home market.

ABOVE RIGHT: *Trilby*: the London Film Company production with Sir Herbert Tree as Svengali and Viva Birkett in the name part. Directed in 1914 by Harold Shaw.

RIGHT: Larry Trimble, directing Alma Taylor and Stewart Rome in *The Awakening of Norah*, a Hepworth production at the Walton studios in 1914.

TOP LEFT: Still, the show must go on as best as it can; this scene was from one of the George Pearson comedies in 1914.

TOP RIGHT: Lovely Jane Gail as Princess Flavia in *The Prisoner of Zenda*.

CENTRE LEFT: *The Prisoner of Zenda* was produced in 1915 by the London Film Company and directed by George Loane Tucker. (L. to r.) Charles Rock as Colonel Sapt, Henry Ainley as Rudolph Rassendyll, Gerald Ames as Rupert of Hentzau (standing) and Arthur Holmes-Gore as Duke Michael.

BOTTOM: The prospect of war must have come as a bitter blow to G. B. Samuelson who had just opened his studio at Worton Hall, Isleworth and about to make his first feature under his own banner. Here cast and crew assemble on Southport Sands for *A Study in Scarlet*, based on the first Sherlock Holmes story and concerning a murder during a Mormon trek in 1850. Samuelson (in boater) is standing with director George Pearson on grass hillock, middle right, 1914.

TOP: 'Was it something I said?' Whatever it was, it was enough for the hand of the law to take its course, the heroine to sob uncontrollably on the hero's shoulder and a lady in the background to fade away with a fit of the vapours.

CENTRE RIGHT: Now, fully recovered, if a little intent, heroine Ruby Miller and our hero Owen Nares, both stars of the period, get to grips with the situation in *Gamblers All*, the tale of a lady gambler who takes the blame for a relative's forgery. Produced at the Samuelson Studios, it was directed by Dave Aylott in 1919.

Jane Shore

Will Barker's leading lady, Blanche Forsythe was cast in the title role of *Jane Shore*, a historical drama based on actual events during the reign of Edward IV. Directed with great skill and shot with imagination by Bert Haldane and F. Martin Thornton in 1915, it was a most ambitious production, employing thousands of extras for crowd scenes. Barker was quickly compared to D. W. Griffiths, and rare for the time, American rights sold equally fast.

CENTRE LEFT: Jane Winstead (Blanche Forsythe) becomes the wife of Matthew Shore (Robert Purdie).
BOTTOM LEFT: King Edward IV (Roy Travers) declares his love for Jane.
BOTTOM RIGHT: Jane is sentenced to do penance.

ABOVE: Lime Grove Studios, Shepherd's Bush 1918. Acquired in 1911/12 by Gaumont, the premises were used as distribution offices only. Production started in the enlarged studios in 1915. Here a set is being prepared for a W. P. Kellino production. The young man on the left of the camera has a fairly confident look about him which is understandable — the world came to know him as Oscar-winning cinematographer Freddie Young.

LEFT: Interior of the Broadwest Film Company's studios at Walthamstow, London, between 1915 and 1922.

TOP RIGHT: By 1920, child actress Chrissie White had grown into a beautiful film star, and, in true show-business style, she went on to marry her leading man, Henry Edwards. Here she is in a scene from *The Amazing Quest of Mr Ernest Bliss*. Also directed by Henry Edwards for Hepworth it sold successfully in America.

TOP LEFT AND BELOW: Posters of *The Amazing Quest of Mr Ernest Bliss*, 1920.

BEHIND THE SCENES IN CINEMA-LAND.

THE RAGE EXHIBITED BY AN AUTHOR WHILE HAVING ONE OF HIS NOVELS FILMED IS UTILISED BY THE INTELLIGENT MANAGER OF THE FILM COMPANY FOR A NEW "THREE-REEL COMIC," ENTITLED "HOW AUTHORS WORK."

Silence is golden?

1920-1929

A VISIT to the cinema in the early 20s was not always the pleasure that it might have been. The entertainment tax that had been introduced during the war was blamed for a number of cinema closures and the deterioration of many picture houses. To be fair, many of the 'bug-hutches' had been in a lousy condition (and one uses that term advisedly) before the tax was introduced. They had, after all, become a retreat for the poor and out of work who, for tuppence a seat (less than half a new penny) could eat their bread and dripping, feed the baby, keep warm and be entertained at the same time. Although the prestigious London and provincial showcase cinemas charged up to 5/9d and 8/6d (about 30-45p) in 1920, average prices ranged from tuppence, fourpence and sevenpence for the cheaper seats up to 2/4d and 3/6d in the better class theatres.

As many picture houses had started life in disused chapels in which the organs were still intact, it became part of the routine entertainment to have an organ 'spot' between films. The audience was encouraged to sing along with the popular melodies of the day, aided by lyrics projected on to the screen. In the meantime, a variety of refreshments — unshelled peanuts, chocolates, cigarettes, even hot tea served from a huge urn strapped to an usherette's chest — would be sold at a brisk and somewhat noisy rate. Later on, of course the organ (very often a Wurlitzer), evolved as an intrinsic part of the cinema programme, rising from the depths of the orchestra pit with its brilliantined player, accompanied by a routine of flashing lights which surrounded them both.

Censorship classification at this time consisted of a U certificate, indicating a film's suitability for general exhibition, and an A certificate, restricting the film to adult entertainment only; 'adult' being defined as 16 years of age and over. Children were only allowed in to see A certificate performances if accompanied by an adult. This regulation allowed any enterprising young cinemagoer who could pass for 16 to gain admittance for the rest of his gang, while an alternative course of action was to approach a total stranger outside the cinema and ask to be accompanied inside.

It was during the 20s that the educational and documentary films came into their own. The highly successful and remarkable series, *Secrets of Nature*, made by Percy Smith and Mary Field for British Instructional Films, and distinguished film-maker John Grierson's *Drifters* in 1929 were landmarks of this genre. Children's programmes also emerged as entertainment in their own right, when Granada Theatres organised the first regular weekly shows for children, making use of films produced for general distribution. It soon became apparent that films should be made specifically for children and in the years to come, J. Arthur Rank would take steps to inaugurate the Children's Film Division within his own company, under the leadership of Mary Field. This Division later developed into the Children's Film Foundation.

New film companies and studios emerged during the 20s while American and French capital investment also became apparent. Paramount opened studios in Islington and made *Road to London* and although the venture did not last long, they were able to give some experience to a hard-working young man in their titles department, Alfred Hitchcock. Gaumont in London also purchased proprietary rights from their parent company in France, thus becoming a British company.

The Minerva Film Company was set up by Adrian Brunel, C. Aubrey Smith and Leslie Howard in 1921 and the new Beaconsfield Studios were opened by George Clark in 1922. Michael Balcon and Victor Saville formed a company and in 1923 produced *Woman to Woman* which showed that hard work had paid off for Alfred Hitchcock, who had been retained by them as assistant director to Graham Cutts. Balcon formed Gainsborough Pictures in 1924 and his first picture, *The Passionate Adventure*, starred Clive Brook and Victor McLaglen. Gainsborough were subsequently absorbed into the Gaumont Picture Corporation in 1928, but still continued to make films at their Islington studios.

Although the Neptune Studios had been founded at Elstree in 1914, it was not until 1927 that this corner of Hertfordshire mushroomed into the British Hollywood. Herbert Wilcox built a large studio there with J. D. Williams in 1926/7 but when financial problems arose, it was purchased by John Maxwell, a clever Scot who renamed it the British International Pictures Studio — BIP. Meanwhile, the former Neptune and Ideal Studios had been purchased by Ludwig Blattner. Herbert Wilcox returned to the fold by opening his British and Dominions Studios next to the BIP lot and the Whitehall Studios — later to become the Gate Studios — had also opened their doors in 1928. Towards the end of the 20s, new studios were opened at Welwyn by British Instructional Films, while the empty Ealing studios were rediscovered by Basil Dean and Sir Gerald du Maurier.

The top stars of the silent screen in the 20s had arrived via the music-hall or the legitimate theatre. Betty Balfour, an impish cockney, with huge blue eyes and golden curls, and Mabel Poulton, another leading lady of the day, both appeared in *Nothing Else Matters* in 1920 and zoomed to stardom. Ivy Duke, Gladys Cooper, Chrissie White, Lilian Hall-Davis, Annette Benson, Alma Taylor, Ruby Miller and Flora le Breton all became darlings of the film fans. On the masculine side Guy Newall, Langhorne Burton, Leslie Howard, Henry Edwards, Ivor Novello, Jack Buchanan, Clive Brook, Victor McLaglen, Brian Aherne, Ian Fleming, Matheson Lang and Jameson Thomas had the ladies shaking in their shimmies, while brilliant clowns like Walter Forde and George Robey played to packed houses.

By the end of 1924, British film production had almost ground to a halt; the old-style British films simply did not compare favourably with the new sophisticated American imports. It must also be remembered that many young men who had undergone some training before the war, and who would at that time have been in their prime, had been killed in action between 1914 and 1918. American product then not only began to dominate British screens, it also seduced the top, but out-of-work British artists to its welcoming shores. Hollywood also made stars out of a number of lesser-known British actors.

Clive Brook, Henry Victor, Ray Milland, Ronald Colman, Leslie Howard and Victor McLaglen were in the main to be lost to the States in the 20s. The romantic English gentleman type never lost his appeal to American audiences, and these gentlemen were to set a standard that was going to be difficult to follow. The British leading ladies, though popular, were never to receive the same rapturous welcome that was afforded to the gallants, although Ruby Miller, Flora le Breton, Dorothy MacKail, Lilian Rich and many others did try their luck on the other side of the water. In the mid-30s, London-born child actor Freddie Bartholomew was to make a tremendous impact on the American public.

Towards the end of the 20s, it became apparent that audiences went to the cinema primarily to see their favourite stars, to whom they felt a very personal attachment. Story lines were not the main attraction, although the romantic and swashbuckling tales provided escapism and glamour and audiences anticipated their visits to the cinema with excitement and pleasure.

For over thirty years the film fans, and the industry, had grown accustomed to screen entertainment — silent screen entertainment, except for the accompanying mood pianist and perhaps the organ recital in the interval. Both audiences and industry were stunned therefore when in 1927 Warner Brothers produced *The Jazz Singer*, with a singing Al Jolson, followed a year later by *The Singing Fool*. The financial, technical and artistic implications of this achievement were enormous and the first reaction of the industry was to close its eyes in the hope that it would go away. Once it was realised, however, that sound was going to be the golden voice of the future, there was fierce competition to be first with a British sound feature film. There were many claims to the title, but Alfred Hitchcock's *Blackmail* made for John Maxwell's BIP studios at Elstree in 1929, is usually regarded by the industry as Britain's entry into sound production. It was the end of one film era and the beginning of another.

Betty Balfour
An impish cockney humour, huge blue eyes and golden curls helped to make Betty Balfour a much loved star of the 20s. She made her first film appearance in 1920 in *Nothing Else Matters*, a Welsh-Pearson production, but is perhaps best remembered for their *Squibs* series.

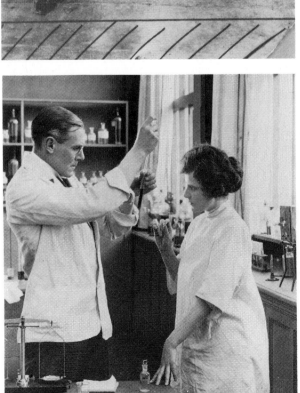

TOP LEFT: Lovely actress Zena Dare appeared in several films in the 20s, but preferred to remain the darling of the theatre.

TOP RIGHT: **Leslie Howard** Born Leslie Stainer to Hungarian immigrants in London in 1893, Howard represented the perfect Englishman, whose wistful, romantic, intellectual looks shot him to stardom — again, not in Britain but in the USA. Adrian Brunel directed Howard and Barbara Hoffe in this 1920 scene from *Five Pounds Reward*, a Minerva production from a story by A. A. Milne.

CENTRE LEFT: Langhorne Burton seems to have noted the error of his ways in Progress Film Company's 1920 production of *Little Dorrit*, directed by Sidney Morgan.

CENTRE RIGHT: Silent screen stars Ivy Duke and Guy Newall were to form a popular partnership when they married in 1922. Franklyn Dyall directed them in *Duke's Son* in 1920.

BOTTOM LEFT: 'That's funny — it was blue a moment ago.' Popular Stewart Rome and Violet Hopson as doctor and nurse in *The Case of Lady Camber*. Based on a comedy thriller play by Horace Vachell, this Broadwest production was directed by Walter West in 1920. Alfred Hitchcock directed Gertrude Lawrence, Gerald du Maurier and Benita Hume in a remake in 1932.

BOTTOM RIGHT: Having received no marked encouragement in England after several years on the London stage and in British film studios, this gentleman departed for America. Lillian Gish then chose him to support her in *The White Sister* in 1929. He went on to become a heart-throb of the 30s and an international star. But in the 1920 Hepworth production of *Anna the Adventuress*, Ronald Colman, seen here with Alma Taylor, must have thought that fame and fortune were a long way off.

TOP LEFT: 'You mean they actually use these for target practice?' Tall stories seem to be the order of the day in *Alf's Button*, Leslie Henson's first film, which also starred Alma Taylor. It was produced and directed by Hepworth in 1920. Hepworth took the adventurous step of sending his two stars to America to promote the film where it did very well.

TOP RIGHT: This 1921 film was directed by Bert Wynne. Holding the bottle is Milton Rosmer.

CENTRE LEFT: *Mary-Find-the-Gold*: a Welsh-Pearson production of 1921, directed by George Pearson and starring Betty Balfour, Hugh E. Wright and Colin Craig (r.). The set, complete with hand-crocheted mats and wash-stand, commands attention.

CENTRE RIGHT: *The Lure of Crooning Water* tells the story of an actress in danger of destroying a farmer's marriage. Produced by George Clark and directed by Arthur Rooke in 1920, the main parts were played by Ivy Duke and Guy Newall.

BOTTOM: **Walter Forde** One of the very few silent comedians of quality in British cinema. During the 20s he appeared in, and later directed, a number of slapstick comedies. There was a sense of loss when he gave up his acting career but by way of compensation, he subsequently directed such successes as *The Ghost Train, Jack's the Boy, Rome Express* and *The Four Just Men.* Here Forde (l.) sacrifices a few fingers when meeting up with George Foley, Pauline Peters and Tom Seymour.

TOP LEFT: **Nora Swinburne** Trained as a ballet dancer, she made her screen debut modelling hats in a Gaumont newsreel. *The Fortune of Christina McNab*, a Gaumont film, was directed in 1921 by Will Kellino, a one-time circus clown and acrobat.

TOP RIGHT: By 1922, film magazines were big business with *Film Weekly* and *Girls' Cinema* the most popular.

ABOVE: Chrissie White and husband Henry Edwards, 1922.

CENTRE LEFT: *Moth and Rust*: Langhorne Burton and Sybil Thorndike (destined to become one of Britain's greatest actresses) are pictured here in a Progress production, directed by Sidney Morgan in 1921.

CENTRE RIGHT: Diana (Betty Faire) tells Bentley (Robert Loraine) of her great love for him in *Bentley's Conscience*. Denison Clift directed in 1922 for Ideal.

BOTTOM: In 1915, David Ivor Davies wrote a patriotic song which became one of the most successful songs of World War I, 'Keep the Home Fires Burning'. After this initial success, Ivor Novello never looked back, becoming a romantic star of the silent screen, composer of popular songs, leading man in West End theatres, successful playwright and actor/manager. He will perhaps be remembered best for two magical Ruritanian musicals, *King's Rhapsody* and *Glamorous Night*. He is seen here in *The Bohemian Girl* (1922) pledging himself to Gladys Cooper while C. Aubrey Smith looks on. Produced by Alliance and directed by Harley Knoles.

TOP LEFT: Gladys Cooper (l.) and the renowned actress Ellen Terry in *The Bohemian Girl.*

TOP RIGHT: J. Stuart Blackton directed this 1922 Stoll production of *The Glorious Adventure.* Pictured (l. to r.) Flora le Breton, the beautiful Lady Diana Manners (later Lady Diana Cooper), and Alice Crawford.

BELOW: Gladys Jennings in *Young Lochinvar.*

CENTRE LEFT: Stoll produced *Young Lochinvar,* based on a poem by Walter Scott, in 1923. Will Kellino directed (l. to r.) Dorothy Harris, Charles Barratt and Cecil Morton York.

SECOND RIGHT: Chrissie White and Henry Edwards in *Boden's Boy,* which Edwards also directed for Hepworth in 1923.

THIRD RIGHT: Jack Buchanan produced *The Fair Maid of Perth,* from a novel by Walter Scott, for Anglia Films at their Beaconsfield Studios in 1923. Edwin Greenwood directed Sylvia Caine and Sydney Paxton.

OPPOSITE: Russell Thorndike in *The Fair Maid of Perth,* 1923. He was a member of the famous theatrical family and brother of Sybil.

BOTTOM LEFT: Flora le Breton and Pedro de Cordoba in *I Will Repay.*

BOTTOM RIGHT: Lewis Gilbert as Merlin questions Juliette (Flora le Breton) and Deroulade (Pedro de Cordoba) in *I Will Repay.* Directed in 1923 by Henry Kolker for Ideal.

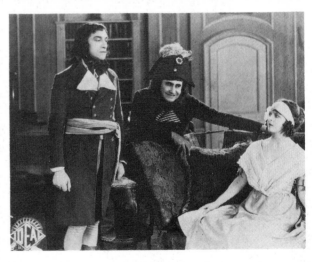

TOP LEFT: A Stoll production of 1923. George Ridgwell directed *Becket*, starring Sir Frank Benson (Becket) seen here preventing Queen Eleanor (Mary Clare) from stabbing Rosamund (Gladys Jennings).

TOP RIGHT: Giving us some sort of clue as to why the Queen wanted to stab the fair Rosamund in the first place. Henry II (A. V. Bramble) visits his mistress Rosamund (Gladys Jennings).

SECOND LEFT: Becket in the presence of King Louis and King Henry in France, demanding that the rights of the church be recognised.

SECOND RIGHT: With the sad result that Henry demands of his knights, 'Who will rid me of this turbulent priest?'

LONG PICTURE: Happy ending at the Emperor's Court. Aladdin (Lionelle Howard, far r.) craves the hand of the Princess (Julia Kean, far l.) from the Emperor (W. Gordon Saunders), while the Widow (popular variety artist George Robey) appears well satisfied with the turn of events in *One Arabian Night*.

BOTTOM LEFT: Julia Kean as Princess of China in Stoll's 1923 production of *One Arabian Night*. Sinclair Hill directed.

BOTTOM RIGHT: A 1923 Edward Godal production of *The Audacious Mr Squire* with (l. to r) Jack Buchanan, Valia, Russell Thorndike, Dorinea Shirley and Malcolm Tod. Edwin Greenwood directed at the B. & C. Studios.

TOP LEFT: Betty Compson and romantic star Clive Brooke in *Woman to Woman*, produced in 1923 by Victor Saville and Michael Balcon. Director Graham Cutts had as his assistant a young Alfred Hitchcock.

CENTRE LEFT: Just deserts? A village scene from *The Gay Corinthian*.

TOP RIGHT: Victor McLaglen and Betty Faire in *The Gay Corinthian*, produced by I. B. Davidson and directed by Arthur Rooke in 1924.

BOTTOM: A telling scene, beautifully lit, from *Decameron Nights.* Here Ivy Duke (Perdita) walks away from Werner Kraus (Soldan). A 1924 Graham-Wilcox production, directed by Herbert Wilcox.

TOP LEFT: *Don Quixote* (1923), directed for Stoll by Maurice Elvey with Jerrold Robertshaw as Don Quixote and George Robey as Sancho Panza.

TOP RIGHT: Ivy Duke pleads with Sessue Hayakawa in a scene from *The Great Prince Shan.* Stoll produced in 1924, A. E. Coleby directed.

CENTRE: One of the figures from *The Dance of the Moods* performed by the Margaret Morris Dancers for the Friese-Greene colour films made at Twickenham Studios and first shown in 1924.

BOTTOM LEFT: *White Slippers.* Matheson Lang tries his hand at reviving Joan Lockton in this 1924 Stoll production, directed by Sinclair Hill.

BOTTOM RIGHT: Produced by Ivor Novello and directed by Adrian Brunel in 1924, *Lovers in Araby* starred Annette Benson and Adrian Brunel. The story, written by Brunel and Miles Mander, is of an engineer rescuing a girl from a bounder while escaping from villains.

The art of the still
Two examples from *The Only Way*, a 1925 Graham-Wilcox production based on *A Tale of Two Cities*, it starred Sir John Martin Harvey as Sydney Carton and was directed by Herbert Wilcox.

TOP LEFT: Leading man of stage and screen Brian Aherne was another British star to find fame in the US, where charming and aristocratic Englishmen were ever popular. He is seen here with Marjorie Hume in the 1925 Stoll production of *The Squire of Long Hadleigh*, directed by Sinclair Hill.

TOP RIGHT: Ivor Novello and Mae Marsh in *The Rat*, produced in 1925 for Gainsborough by Michael Balcon and directed by Graham Cutts.

ABOVE: Fred Paul, actor and director, seen here in *The Last Witness*. Paul also directed this film for Stoll in 1925.

CENTRE: *She* (1925). A courageous attempt by G. B. Samuelson to bring H. Rider Haggard's novel to the screen. Directed by Leander de Cordova, it was shot mainly in Berlin. Cast and crew assemble for a publicity shot, cheered on by Mr and Mrs G. B. Samuelson (bottom right).

BOTTOM: *Tale of a Tendril*, 1925. This is one of the many very successful 'Secrets of Nature' films made by British Instructional from the one-time Neptune studios at Borehamwood.

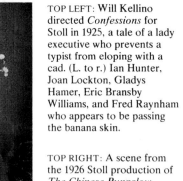

TOP LEFT: Will Kellino directed *Confessions* for Stoll in 1925, a tale of a lady executive who prevents a typist from eloping with a cad. (L. to r.) Ian Hunter, Joan Lockton, Gladys Hamer, Eric Bransby Williams, and Fred Raynham who appears to be passing the banana skin.

TOP RIGHT: A scene from the 1926 Stoll production of *The Chinese Bungalow*, directed by Sinclair Hill and starring (l. to r.) Matheson Lang, Juliette Compton and Genevieve Townsend.

CENTRE LEFT: Steering a humorous course for the crew of *HMS Determination* seems to be something of a chore for Moore Marriott (centre) in this 1926 Dinah Shury production of *Second to None*. Jack Raymond directed.

CENTRE RIGHT: A little late for a change of heart for Ian Fleming and Benita Hume in *Second to None*.

BOTTOM: Ivor Novello and June in *The Lodger*, made for Gainsborough in 1926. Up and coming director Alfred Hitchcock revealed an early taste for the macabre in this tale based on the Jack the Ripper murders.

TOP AND CENTRE RIGHT:
Every picture tells a story . . .
Scenes from *Sahara Love*
with Marie Colette, Gordon
Hopkirk (centre) and John
Dehelly as the undoubted
hero. Produced by Stoll in
1926 and directed by Sinclair
Hill.

BOTTOM LEFT AND RIGHT:
Director Graham Cutts had
two of the most popular film
personalities of the 20s to
head the cast of *Confetti*,
Annette Benson and Jack
Buchanan. A romantic story,
set in Nice, of a duchess
attempting to divert her
nephew's affections to
another lady, it was made for
First-National at
Twickenham in 1927.

'CONFETTI'
A First National British Picture.

'CONFETTI'

ABOVE: In 1927 John Maxwell gained control of the British National Studios at Elstree, renaming them British International Pictures Ltd. The British film industry will always owe a debt of gratitude to this canny, clever Scot who had the vision and courage to invest his skills and money in the pursuit of its development. It would also, no doubt, have given him a certain satisfaction to know that nearly 60 years on this studio, now Thorn-EMI Elstree Studios, is headed by another clever, canny Scot, Andrew Mitchell.

TOP: BIP Studios, *c.* 1927.

CENTRE: Scene from *Thou Fool*, directed by Fred Paul for Stoll in 1926.

BOTTOM: Alfred Hitchcock was now working for John Maxwell at the BIP Studios at Elstree and in 1927 made *The Ring*, a technically impressive silent film about two prize-fighters and their rivalry in the ring and romance. It starred (l. to r.) Gordon Harker, Carl Brisson and Harry Terry. The film was well received by the critics.

OPPOSITE: Lilian Hall-Davis played the role of Madeleine in the Gaumont British 1927 release *Roses of Picardy*. Maurice Elvey directed and co-produced with Victor Saville.

TOP LEFT: A scene from *Roses of Picardy*.

TOP RIGHT: Noel Coward visits the set of *The Vortex* in 1927 to see how the filming of his play is progressing. (L. to r.) Noel Coward, Ivor Novello, Allan Holles, Willette Kershaw, Frances Doble. Director Adrian Brunel looks on from the back of the settee. *The Vortex* was produced by Michael Balcon for Gainsborough.

CENTRE LEFT: *Rolling Road* (1927).

BOTTOM LEFT: Carlyle Blackwell and Flora le Breton in *Rolling Road*, co-produced by Blackwell/Balcon under the direction of Graham Cutts.

CENTRE RIGHT: *A Woman Redeemed*. Sinclair Hill directed James Carew and Stella Arbenina in this 1927 production for Stoll.

BOTTOM RIGHT: Matheson Lang and Joan Lockton in *The King's Highway*, the 1927 Stoll production directed by Sinclair Hill.

TOP LEFT: *Blighty*, directed by Adrian Brunel for Gainsborough in 1927. Godfrey Winn bids farewell to his mother (Ellaline Terriss) and sister (Lilian Hall-Davis) on his way to the Front.

TOP RIGHT: *Blighty*.

BELOW: The aim of the trifle-stuffing Nero does not seem to correspond with that of the gentleman at his rear. A scene from Gaumont's *What Money Can Buy*.

CENTRE RIGHT: Madeleine Carroll finds support in the pillar of the church while John Longden (l.) and Humberston Wright await the outcome in *What Money Can Buy*, produced in 1928 by Maurice Elvey and directed by Edwin Greenwood.

BOTTOM RIGHT: Captain John Heritage (Pat Aherne) prepares to defend Princess Saskia (Vera Voronina) from her enemies in *Huntingtower*, from the novel by John Buchan. A Welsh-Pearson production of 1927, directed by George Pearson.

BOTTOM LEFT: Ray Milland in the 20s, before he left Britain to further his career in Hollywood.

TOP LEFT: Ivor Novello and Mabel Poulton starred in this 1928 Balcon production of *The Constant Nymph*, directed by Adrian Brunel.

CENTRE LEFT: Nobody asked him to play, and it certainly does not look as if Frances Doble (l.) and Elsa Lanchester are about to make amends to Ivor Novello in *The Constant Nymph.*

TOP RIGHT: *Dawn*, 1928, produced and directed by Herbert Wilcox. Sybil Thorndike, seen here with Maurice Bradell, gave a memorable performance as Nurse Cavell. The film tells of her arrest, trial and subsequent execution for helping 210 men to escape to England at the beginning of World War I.

BOTTOM: Hermione Baddeley watches anxiously as Bobby Howes is in danger of losing his balance whilst proposing a victory toast in *Guns of Loos.*

BELOW: **Madeleine Carroll** Born in West Bromwich, she gave up a teaching career to try her luck as an actress in London. Her true English beauty was quickly spotted by agents who launched her in films. Here she is seen making her debut in Stoll's 1928 production of *Guns of Loos* with Henry Victor which Sinclair Hill directed.

TOP: One could ask if the lady second from right suffers from bunions, or if she just likes wearing odd slippers, or if the pigeon under the table is part of the act, or indeed if John Longden and Alf Goddard (with battered bowler) should not have spent a bit more time getting it together in the first place. Doubtless it is all part of the illusion as Estelle Brody prepares for her mummification in *Mademoiselle Parley-Voo*, directed by Maurice Elvey for Gaumont in 1928.

BELOW: Tears as well as *Champagne* for Betty Balfour in this BIP production, directed by Alfred Hitchcock in 1928.

CENTRE LEFT: Dorothy (later Chili) Bouchier met with great success in this 1928 BIF presentation, directed by Anthony Asquith in which Brian Aherne co-starred.

BOTTOM LEFT: Chili Bouchier and Harry Milton. A popular theatrical partnership. Chili (Dorothy) Bouchier was given the part of a bathing beauty in Asquith's film *Shooting Stars*, followed by a contract with Herbert Wilcox's British and Dominions Studios. She met Harry Milton (whose brother Billy was also in films) in 1928 while he was making his screen debut and they married in 1929.

BOTTOM RIGHT: A 'Lux' advertisement, 1929. Courtesy of Unilever plc.

BIF Production   "SHOOTING STARS"   New Era Distribution
BY ANTHONY ASQUITH

On the Stage and Screen ‥

Stars keep their stockings beautiful with LUX

TOP LEFT: (L. to r.) Alf Goddard, Enid Stamp-Taylor, Hayford Hobbs, Olive Rimmer, Captain R. Davis MP, and Violet Hopson on the set of *Remembrance*, directed by Bert Wynne, produced by Sidney Eaton in 1928.

TOP RIGHT: Neither inebriation nor make-up brush were responsible for the lines on the noses of Betty Balfour and Syd Chaplin in *A Little Bit of Fluff*, the BIP comedy of 1928, directed by Jess Robins. They were in fact an indication from the head of the stills department that the proboscidean charms of both artists were not quite what they should be and could something please be done about them . . . in photographic terms.

CENTRE: Alf Goddard (l.) and Cyril McLaglen are the rival mates whose conflicting interests give rise to most of the action in the Gaumont British screen comedy *You Know What Sailors Are*, directed in 1928 by Maurice Elvey.

CENTRE RIGHT: Cast and crew of *The Farmer's Wife*, directed for BIP in 1929 by Alfred Hitchcock, crouched next to the aproned Lilian Hall-Davis. Also starring in this tale of a widowed farmer seeking a new bride is Jameson Thomas (standing, with watch-chain).

BOTTOM: Child actor Kenneth Rive (later to head Gala Films) in a scene with Mary Odette in the BIP production of *Emerald of the East*, directed in 1929 by Jean de Kuharski.

TOP LEFT: A scene from BIP's *Widecombe Fair* directed in 1928 by Norman Walker at Elstree Studios. This Devon romance starred Marguerite Allen, Wyndham Standing, Violet Hopson and William Freshman.

TOP RIGHT: It was here a moment ago. . . . Cyril McLaglen in *The Lost Patrol*, directed by Walter Summers for BIF in 1929.

SECOND LEFT: Directed by Arthur Maude in 1929, Benita Hume and Donald Calthrop starred in *The Clue of the New Pin*, made by British Lion Film Corporation, which was formed in 1927. They acquired Beaconsfield Studios along with the film rights of the works of Edgar Wallace who also became chairman of the company. Production manager of the studios was Percy Nash, who had helped to found the Neptune Studios at Elstree in 1914.

THIRD LEFT: Heartthrob Jameson Thomas and Isobel Jeans in the 1929 British Filmcraft production *Power Over Men*, directed by George Banfield.

BOTTOM LEFT: Robert Irvin in *A Knight in London*.

BOTTOM RIGHT:
Lilian Harvey
London born, she became a star in England and Germany where she had been forced to remain at the outbreak of World War I. She is seen here waiting for *A Knight in London*, directed by Lupu Pick in 1929 for Ludwig Blattner.

WILLIAM FOX Presents "THE LOST PATROL" with Cyril McLaglen

TOP RIGHT:
Sir Harry Lauder
The much-loved music-hall entertainer, born in Edinburgh in 1870, is seen here keeping his spirits up in *Auld Lang Syne* made by Welsh-Pearson in 1929 and directed by George Pearson.

TOP LEFT: Returning the compliment: Dodo Watts, Pat Aherne and Dorothy Boyd in *Auld Lang Syne*.

CENTRE LEFT AND BOTTOM: Before and after: Bernard Nedell cleans up while the doctors groan in despair over Ivor Novello who, it appears, might recover. *The Return of the Rat*, a Balcon production, directed in 1929 by Graham Cutts.

ABOVE: Gordon Harker in *The Return of the Rat*.

Sound! Sound! Sound!

TOP: Anxious director Alfred Hitchcock on the set of *Blackmail*, testing star Anny Ondra's voice for quality. Unfortunately, her Czech accent combined with early recording systems to give a totally incomprehensible noise. Joan Barry was called in to dub the star's voice at the side of the set while Ondra mouthed the words.

BOTTOM: John Longden (l.), Anny Ondra and Donald Calthrop in a scene from *Blackmail*.

BELOW: Amid fierce competition, the BIP production *Blackmail* emerged as what is usually regarded as Britain's first talkie in 1929.

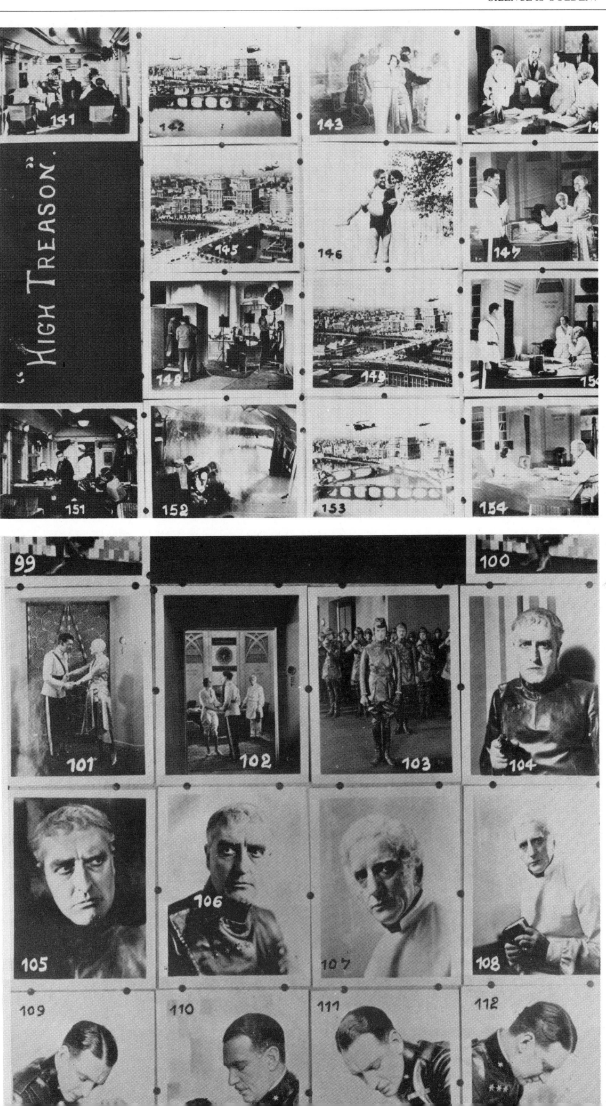

TOP AND BOTTOM: Scenes of London in the 40s as visualised in *High Treason*, made in 1929. In the foreground, Waterloo Bridge; beyond, the new Charing Cross Bridge, at the foot of which is the League of Peace Building. Other scenes include the making of the film and its stars — Humbertson Wright, Jameson Thomas and Benita Hume. *High Treason* was Gaumont's first talking feature film and was directed by Maurice Elvey. Sets, costumes and special effects were all considered ahead of their time, but perhaps the most interesting feature is the story line — about a group of women uniting to prevent financiers from engineering a second world war.

BELOW: Publicity for an advertising film from *The Co-operative News* (1929).

ELEGANCE

Great care in design and thoroughness in manufacture make DESBEAU the most graceful foundation for dainty dresses that high-class corsetry can offer.

Made under Trade Union conditions in an ideal factory.

C.W.S.

DESBEAU CORSETS

Sold by Co-operative Societies Only.

SAY "C.W.S."

TOP LEFT: John Longden breaks the bleak news to Monty Banks in *Atlantic*.

TOP RIGHT: Another success for BIP Elstree was *Atlantic*, the story of the *Titanic*, directed in 1929 by E. A. Dupont. Here, John Stuart and Madeleine Carroll face the music in lighthearted fashion before the news is revealed that the ship is sinking.

ABOVE: There was speedy promotion for English Rose Madeleine Carroll, seen here with Carl Brisson in *The American Prisoner*, made by BIP in 1929, and directed by Thomas Bentley.

BOTTOM: A scene during the production of the 1929 film *The City of Play*, directed from one of his own stories by Denison Clift for Michael Balcon at Gainsborough.

The booming thirties

1930-1939

BECAUSE AMERICAN competition had affected British film production and therefore exhibition of its product, the 1928 British Cinematograph Films Act stipulated that both renters and exhibitors had to fulfil an annually increasing quota of British films over 3000 feet in length. This particular Act expired in 1938, but during the ten years it prevailed, it led to the making of many 'quota quickies'. These were films made cheaply and quickly, simply to fulfil quota regulations, and many poor films were churned out in the process. The positive side of the Act meant that British production boomed, studios and artists were kept busy, and American investment and interest in British production increased. The boom also gave many unknown actors and technicians the opportunity to learn their craft, and at regular intervals, a worthwhile 'quota quickie' or new star would emerge.

Although the decade started slowly in production terms, it rapidly gained momentum and became a golden era for British cinema. A contradiction in terms when one thinks of the 'quota quickies' perhaps, but in fact it was a period during which many of our finest directors and cinematographers as well as stars, developed and expanded their techniques and talents. At the same time, gutsy and imaginative production heads like Michael Balcon, John Maxwell, J. Arthur Rank, Herbert Wilcox and Hungarian born Alexander Korda all made their own contribution to British production and, in some cases, to exhibition.

The cinemas also boomed in the 30s as funds poured into exhibition and audiences increased. John Maxwell's Associated British Picture Corporation, as it was now called, owned 120 cinemas in 1930 which had increased to 325 in 1938. The Gaumont-British Picture Corporation controlled 287 cinemas in 1930 while the Odeon circuit, later controlled by J. Arthur Rank, had 250 cinemas by 1937.

Among the now legendary names to emerge as directors in the decade were: Anthony Asquith with his first sound film *Tell England*, released in 1931; Carol Reed, who had started his career as dialogue director and released his first independent feature *Midshipman Easy* in 1935; Michael Powell, attracting attention with *The Edge of the World* in 1937, starring Niall MacGinnis, Belle Chrystal, John Laurie and Finlay Currie; and David Lean, who served his apprenticeship as a cutter on 'quota quickies', going on to edit such films as *Pygmalion* and *French Without Tears*, before making his directorial debut, some years later, with Noel Coward on *In Which We Serve*. *Blackmail* had already established Alfred Hitchcock's reputation as a director.

It was not just technical or directorial problems that confronted the industry with the arrival of sound. Screen actors had to have a voice, a good voice, which meant clear quality and diction to combat the early recording systems — and certainly no accents, cockney or continental. Consequently a number of artists fell by the wayside; the real tragedy, however, was for the silent comedian whose art could never be the same again.

Thus a new breed of film comedy player emerged for the new-style comedies. Cicely Courtneidge and Jack Hulbert, Will Hay, Ernie Lotinga and Will Fyffe now appeared regularly in light comedies while the popular Aldwych Farces such as *Rookery Nook* transferred very successfully to the screen with their stars Tom Walls, Ralph Lynn, Robertson Hare and Winifred Shotter. Leslie Fuller made twenty low-budget comedies including *Why Sailors Leave Home, The Last Coupon* and *My Wife's Family*. Arthur Lucan (Old Mother Riley), Max Miller and Tommy Trinder appeared in the latter part of the decade. The sound of music also came in with the talkies, but now it was on the screen. It was natural, then, that singing should follow, producing a galaxy of musical comedy stars — Jack Buchanan and Anna Neagle in *Goodnight Vienna*, Jessie Matthews kicking shapely legs over her shoulder in *Evergreen*, Gracie Fields — the Lassie from Lancashire — in *Sing As We Go* and toothy, banjo-playing comedian George Formby. West End stars Elsie Randolph, Gene Gerrard, Evelyn Laye and Bobby Howes also became very popular at the cinema box-office.

During the time when British stars were being feted in the States, shrewd British production heads were importing their American and continental counterparts to British shores. John Maxwell coaxed Raquel Torres and Charles Bickford over for *Red Wagon*, Douglas Fairbanks Junior for *Mimi*, Bebe Daniels for *A Southern Maid* and Ben Lyon to star in his production of *I Spy*, along with Buddy Rogers for *Let's Make a Night of It*. Other producers inveigled Marlene Dietrich, Esther Ralston, Conrad Veidt, Robert Taylor, Lionel Barrymore and Maureen O'Sullivan.

Several British studios were either opened or rebuilt during these boom years. In 1930 the new Ealing studios were opened by Basil Dean and Stephen and Jack Courtauld. Director Monty Banks left BIP in 1935 to work at Ealing and Michael Balcon took over there from Basil Dean in 1938. Norman Louden opened Sound City at Shepperton in 1933 and was joined by John Baxter. Baxter made many quota quickies at Shepperton including *Birds of a Feather* and *Flood Tide* which, although low on budget, were rich in sentiment. Lime Grove Studios, rebuilt in 1932, were officially reopened in 1933. Three years later, Pinewood Studios, soon to be headed by J. Arthur Rank, opened their doors to welcome, among others, Herbert Wilcox, whose British and Dominions Studios at Elstree had been gutted by fire. A few miles away, Alexander Korda opened Denham Studios for his London Films Production and for a period of time Julius Hagen had under his control studios at Twickenham, Hammersmith and Elstree, whilst the Soskin family completed their Amalgamated Studios at Elstree in 1937.

In that same year, Two Cities Films were set up by Filippo del Giudice and Charter Films were formed by the Boulting Brothers, Roy and John. The Americans also acquired a firm footing in British production. Warner Brothers and First-National now owned studios at Teddington, 20th Century-Fox were installed at Wembley, while Columbia, Paramount, United Artists and Universal all had British production affiliations.

Of the films and stars in the 30s, it must be said that Alexander Korda's contribution to the British film industry was a major achievement. With *The Private Life of Henry VIII*, he produced Britain's first really effective answer to world competition and with it captured the American box-office. *The Scarlet Pimpernel, Things to Come, Rembrandt, Fire Over England, Knight Without Armour, The Drum* and *The Four Feathers* were all made by him, and his stars included Binnie Barnes, Robert Donat, Leslie Howard, Elsa Lanchester, Gertrude Lawrence, Charles Laughton, Vivien Leigh, Raymond Massey, Merle Oberon, Laurence Olivier, Ralph Richardson and Flora Robson.

Producer Herbert Wilcox was another studio head to whom the British cinema will always owe a debt of gratitude. A great showman, he was responsible for films such as *Goodnight Vienna, Bitter Sweet, Nell Gwyn, Peg of Old Drury, Victoria the Great* and *Sixty Glorious Years* all starring Anna Neagle, which had great appeal to mass audiences.

As the 30s drew to a close, the new British Cinematograph Films Act of 1938, which had reduced the British quotas for cinemas and renters, began adversely to affect film production. But an even greater threat was looming over Britain and Europe in 1939 when the Second World War was declared. In many ways it was back to 1914 all over again.

By 1931 Ealing Studios, which had been founded by film pioneer Will Barker just after the turn of the century, had new owners, the Associated Talking Pictures (ATP), with Basil Dean, Sir Gerald du Maurier, Stephen Courtauld and Reginald Baker at its helm. They acquired property adjoining the old studios and proceeded to build the new Ealing Studios — the first purpose-built in Britain.

TOP LEFT: In 1929, Julius Hagen formed the Twickenham Film Studios with Leslie Hiscott and Henry Edwards, taking over the old St Margaret's studios. One of their films, released in 1930, was *The Call of the Sea*, starring Bernard Nedell (l.), Chili Bouchier and Henry Edwards. Hiscott directed this Hagen/Edwards production.

TOP RIGHT: Leading comedian Sydney Howard made his first stage appearance in 1912 and went on to appear in a number of films including *French Leave*, produced in 1930 by D. & H. Productions and directed by Jack Raymond.

CENTRE LEFT: Tom Walls and colleagues decided that the successful Aldwych Farces would transfer very well to the screen. They became a cult in the 30s. Seen here in *Rookery Nook*, reviewing the situation are (l. to r.) Tom Walls, Robertson Hare, Winifred Shotter and Ralph Lynn, who always played the 'silly ass'. Like many of these farces, the scenario was written by Ben Travers, based on his own stage play and directed by Tom Walls for Herbert Wilcox at his B. & D. Elstree Studios, in 1930.

BOTTOM: Unpopular with the critics, but successful at the box office was *Murder*, directed for BIP by Alfred Hitchcock in 1930. Its popularity was probably due to handsome, one-legged Herbert Marshall (seen here with Norah Baring), another British thespian to become a star in American talkies.

TOP LEFT: Evidently not *A Warm Corner* for Austin Melford and Heather Thatcher in this story, set on the Riviera, of a cornplaster millionaire who is blackmailed for flirting with a married lady. A Gainsborough production by Balcon and directed by Victor Saville in 1930.

TOP RIGHT: *The Chinese Bungalow* (1930): Jill Esmond made her film debut in this Neo-Art remake by J. B. Williams and Arthur W. Barnes. Seen here with Derek Williams and Matheson Lang (r.)

CENTRE RIGHT: Edna Best and Miles Mander, two British stars of the 30s, seen here in *Loose Ends*, produced by BIP in 1930. Best married Herbert Marshall in 1929, but unlike her husband did not manage to further her career in the USA. Former sheep farmer Mander tried aviation, motor-racing, writing and film renting before making his film debut in crowd scenes, then becoming an actor and director.

BOTTOM: *Harmony Heaven*, 1930. The first British film made as a talkie in colour, it starred Polly Ward, Stuart Hall, Trilby Clark and Jack Raine. Another first for the Elstree Studios of BIP, the film was directed by Thomas Bentley.

TOP: **They Don't Make Films Like That Any More**
Dorothy Seacombe, the heroine, with full supporting cast rings down the curtain on Warwick Ward, the villain, in *The Yellow Mask*, directed by Harry Lachman for BIP in 1930.

BOTTOM: **They Don't Make Films Like That Any More, Part II**
Leslie Fuller in the 1930 BIP comedy *Kiss Me Sergeant*, directed by Monty Banks.

TOP: A scene from the BIP production of *Night Birds*, directed by Richard Eichberg in 1930.

BOTTOM LEFT: Former music hall artist Herbert Mundin as Lady Isabel and Alf Goddard as the man in her life, in the Gaumont burlesque of 1931 directed by George Pearson, *East Lynne on the Western Front*. It tells the story of a platoon of soldiers who decide to stage their comedy version of 'East Lynne', while billeted in an empty theatre.

CENTRE RIGHT: Rehearsal call in *East Lynne on the Western Front*.

BOTTOM RIGHT: '**I want you two to be friends . . .**' Carl Brisson (l.), Edna Davies and Henry Victor in *Song of Soho*, directed in 1930 for BIP by Harry Lachman.

TOP: *Why Sailors Leave Home* (1930). Looking as if he would be happy to return as soon as possible is Leslie Fuller, in this BIP production, directed by Monty Banks. Fuller was one of the many music hall comedians recruited during the 30s to appear in British films, along with such artists as Will Fyffe, Will Hay, Ernie Lotinga, Arthur Lucan, Kitty McShane, Max Miller, Herbert Mundin, Tommy Trinder and many more.

CENTRE LEFT: On set of *The Great Game* (l. to r.) Randle Ayrton, Neil Kenyon, Kenneth Cove and Renee Clama. Directed by Jack Raymond for Gaumont in 1930.

BOTTOM LEFT: Tea for two in *Raise the Roof* with ever popular Betty Balfour and Jack Raine in a BIP film, directed in 1930 by Walter Summers.

BOTTOM RIGHT:
Gracie Fields
The lassie from Lancashire began her career in the cotton mills, making her music hall debut in Rochdale in 1911. She went on to become a much-loved singer and comedienne of stage and screen. Her plucky and cheeky personality on screen did much to enliven the years of depression in the 30s. She became the highest paid actress of the period, as well as the top box-office draw. During a serious illness, a newspaper cartoon spread across the front page said it all in two words — 'Our Gracie'.

TOP LEFT: Belle Chrystal and Edmund Gwenn in *Hindle Wakes*, a Gaumont picture produced by Michael Balcon and directed by Victor Saville in 1931.

TOP RIGHT: Looks like the end of the line for *The Ghost Train* cast (l. to r.) Tracy Holmes, Carol Coombe, Cyril Raymond, Jack Hulbert, Ann Todd and Cicely Courtneidge. A Balcon production for Gainsborough, directed by Walter Forde in 1931.

ABOVE: Tony Bruce in *Tell England*.

CENTRE: A 1931 British Instructional Films production about the Gallipoli campaign, *Tell England* was Anthony Asquith's first sound film.

BOTTOM LEFT: Henry Kendall and Joan Barry in *Rich and Strange*, directed by Alfred Hitchcock for BIP in 1931.

BOTTOM RIGHT: Bertie Samuelson (r.) boarding a train for the French Riviera with stars Wendy Barrie and Gerald Rawlinson for *Collision*, a 'quota quickie' (a film made quickly in order to comply with the regulation percentage of British film quota exhibited at British cinemas). Directed by E. Gordon Craig in 1931.

'TELL ENGLAND.'

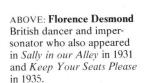

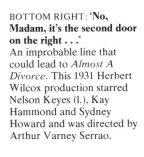

TOP: Syd Courteney, Leslie Fuller and the American star-to-be Peter Lawford, (the seven-year-old son of General Sir Sydney and Lady Crawford) with Iris Ashley in *Poor Old Bill*, a BIP featurette made in 1931, directed by Monty Banks.

CENTRE LEFT: *The Love Habit* with Walter Armitage (l.), Seymour Hicks and Elsa Lanchester, a 1931 BIP film directed by Harry Lachman.

CENTRE RIGHT: **'If I could plant a tiny seed of love . . .'** Garry Marsh and Margot Grahame in the 1931 BIP production of *Uneasy Virtue*, directed by Norman Walker.

BOTTOM LEFT: Clifford Heatherley appears to be supported by a number of young Chinese fans and looks inscrutably content in *My Old China*, produced by Michael Balcon for Gainsborough in 1931, and directed by W. P. Kellino.

ABOVE: **Florence Desmond** British dancer and impersonator who also appeared in *Sally in our Alley* in 1931 and *Keep Your Seats Please* in 1935.

BOTTOM RIGHT: **'No, Madam, it's the second door on the right . . .'** An improbable line that could lead to *Almost A Divorce*. This 1931 Herbert Wilcox production starred Nelson Keyes (l.), Kay Hammond and Sydney Howard and was directed by Arthur Varney Serrao.

TOP: *Dreyfus* with Cedric Hardwicke in the name part, seen here with Beatrice Thomson. This version of the much-filmed story of a Jewish officer falsely convicted of spying in 1894, was directed by Milton Rosmer for BIP in 1931.

CENTRE RIGHT: Edmund Gwenn, C. V. France and Jill Esmond played in *The Skin Game*, a story of blackmail and intrigue directed by Alfred Hitchcock for BIP in 1931.

BELOW: Ben Webster, born in 1864, was a stage and screen actor of some renown, and married to Dame May Whitty. He is seen here in *The Lyons Mail*, a Julius Hagen production directed by Arthur Maude in 1931 at the Twickenham Studios. His many films included *Bootle's Baby, The Vicar of Wakefield, The Call of Youth* and *The Old Curiosity Shop*.

BOTTOM LEFT: George Thirwell in *The Lyons Mail*.

BOTTOM RIGHT: Ronald Frankau seems unaware that he is in the hot seat as he receives the full treatment from rose-tickling Muriel Angelus assisted by Gene Gerrard in *Let's Love and Laugh*, a BIP production directed by Richard Eichberg in 1931.

TOP LEFT: Anne Grey and John Stuart caught in a tense situation in Alfred Hitchcock's thriller *Number Seventeen*, produced by BIP in 1932.

TOP RIGHT: A scene from *Bull Rushes*, produced by Michael Balcon at the Gainsborough Studios and directed by W. P. Kellino in 1931.

CENTRE RIGHT: Lovely, up-and-coming star of the 30s and onwards, Anna Neagle is seen here with Henry Edwards in *The Flag Lieutenant*, produced by her husband-to-be Herbert Wilcox and directed in 1932 by Henry Edwards.

BOTTOM: Foyer still of *The First Mrs Fraser*, which might have been more aptly titled 'The Sensible Mr Fraser', since this Sterling production of 1932 is the story of a rich man returning to his first wife on learning that his second wife is loved by a younger man. Direction was by Sinclair Hill and the film starred Henry Ainley, Joan Barry and Dorothy Dix.

TOP LEFT: Looking remarkably like a scene from *Death on the Nile* — made in the 70s — is a shot from *Fires of Fate*, produced in 1932 by BIP at Elstree and directed by Norman Walker. It starred Clifford Heatherley, Jean Cadell and Hubert Harben.

TOP RIGHT: *Fires of Fate*: Kathleen O'Regan basks in the undisguised admiration of (l. to r.) Lester Matthews, Hubert Harben, Donald Calthrop and Jack Raine.

CENTRE LEFT: Henry Kendall (r.) may have received the key of the door but a build-up of neighbourly tensions seems inevitable when confronted by Sam Livesey in *Mr Bill the Conqueror*, directed by Norman Walker for BIP in 1932.

CENTRE RIGHT: Arthur Wontner as Sherlock Holmes in a scene from *The Missing Rembrandt*, produced in Twickenham by Julius Hagen in 1932, directed by Leslie Hiscott. Ian Fleming played Dr Watson. Minnie Rayner is in attendance.

BOTTOM LEFT: Bobby Howes, musical star of the 30s, appeared in a number of films including *Guns of Loos* and *Third Time Lucky*. Father of Sally Ann Howes, a child star who also rose to stardom on stage and screen. *Lord Babs*, made for Gainsborough by Michael Balcon in 1932, was directed by Walter Forde.

BOTTOM RIGHT: Leslie Fuller and Mary Jerrold in *The Last Coupon*, directed by Thomas Bentley for BIP in 1932.

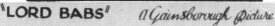

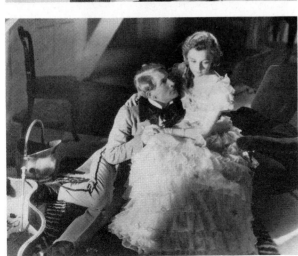

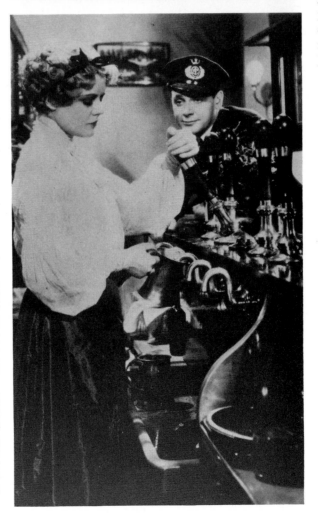

TOP LEFT: Esther Ralston and Hugh Williams in *Rome Express*, made at the newly built Lime Grove studios. One of the successes of 1932, it was directed by Walter Forde and produced by Michael Balcon.

TOP RIGHT: The Gaumont Lime Grove studios, Shepherd's Bush, rebuilt in 1932. Over £500,000 was spent on building and re-equipping.

SECOND LEFT: '**I prefer the one with sequins . . .**' Gordon Harker and Leonora Corbett in a scene from *Love on Wheels* (1932), a Michael Balcon production directed by Victor Saville. The cast also included Roland Culver, Martita Hunt and Miles Malleson all at the beginning of their careers.

CENTRE RIGHT: '**But I get seasick on a loose floor-board . . .**' Ernie Lotinga (in trilby) turns a deaf ear to the pleas of Jack Frost (l.) in *Josser Joins the Navy*, one of a series of popular comedies. This one was directed by Norman Lee for BIP in 1932.

THIRD LEFT: (L. to r.) Kenneth Cove, Muriel Aked and Harry Tate in *Her First Affair* (1932), produced by Frank Richardson and directed by Allan Dwan.

BOTTOM LEFT: Carl Harbord and Ann Casson in *Dance Pretty Lady* directed by Anthony Asquith for BIF in this 1932 H. Bruce Woolfe production from a story by Compton Mackenzie.

BOTTOM RIGHT: Husband and wife team Herbert Marshall and Edna Best in *The Faithful Heart*, a Gainsborough picture from Michael Balcon, directed by Victor Saville in 1932.

117-26

OPPOSITE:

Gertrude Lawrence
Born in London in 1898, she made her first stage appearance at the age of ten in *Dick Whittington* and went on to become a musical comedy star. A wilful, extravagant cockney sprite, she had that indefinable star quality and an immense physical magnetism which attracted royalty, fellow-artists and Joe Public in the 'gods' alike. This magical quality did not transfer itself to the screen, however, and she is perhaps best known for her stage performances in plays such as *Private Lives*, specially written for her by Noel Coward.

ABOVE: Gertie Lawrence in a scene from *Lord Camber's Ladies*, watched by Alfred Hitchcock from the stalls. Hitchcock produced and Benn W. Levy directed for BIP in 1932.

LEFT: Hugh Williams and Elizabeth Allan in a scene from the Paramount British picture *Insult*. This French Foreign Legion tale was directed in 1932 by Harry Lachman at the Imperial Studios in Elstree. Sam Livesey (l.) and John Gielgud are in the background.

TOP LEFT: (L. to r.) Norah Howard, Gordon Harker, Edmund Gwenn, Jane Welsh and Cyril Raymond in the 1932 thriller *Condemned to Death*, made by Julius Hagen at Twickenham and directed by Walter Forde.

ABOVE: Wendy Barrie was chosen by Alexander Korda for her first major part in *Wedding Rehearsal*, produced and directed by him in 1932. A long-term contract with Korda's London Film Productions followed.

TOP RIGHT: Barry Jones and Anne Grey in *Arms and the Man*. A 1932 BIP production, directed by Cecil Lewis, this was something of a coup for John Maxwell who had acquired the film rights from George Bernard Shaw.

CENTRE RIGHT: British actor George Curzon and American leading lady Esther Ralston teamed up in *After the Ball*, produced by Michael Balcon for Gaumont in 1932 and directed by Milton Rosmer.

BOTTOM: A scene from *In a Monastery Garden*, produced by Julius Hagen at Twickenham and directed in 1932 by Maurice Elvey.

'IN A MONASTERY GARDEN'

ABOVE AND INSET: Seen here on location with Tamara Desni in 1932 is boxer-turned-actor Jack Doyle for *McGlusky the Sea Rover*, a BIP tale of gun-running and Arabs directed by Walter Summers with production by Walter Mycroft.

Goodnight Vienna
This 1932 musical romance set in Vienna in 1913 and directed and produced by Herbert Wilcox at the British and Dominions Studios, Elstree, marked the beginning of the 46-year partnership between Wilcox and Anna Neagle.

LEFT: Shades of *My Fair Lady* — Anna Neagle and Joyce Bland

CENTRE RIGHT: Jack Buchanan and Anna Neagle. Matinee idol Buchanan scored a particular success for his rendering of the title song, still laden with nostalgia for anyone born between the two World Wars.

BOTTOM RIGHT: Wilcox and Buchanan on set.

TOP: *Lucky Girl* as seen by cameraman Bryan Langley. Molly Lamont, standing between Gus McNaughton (spectacled) and Gene Gerrard looks lucky indeed if the general toasting is anything to go by. A BIP production, directed by Gene Gerrard and Frank Miller in 1932.

Tonight's the Night
Directed for BIP by Monty Banks in 1932.

SECOND LEFT: Before: Leslie Fuller seems intent on persuading the visiting entertainers to audition his hidden talents.

CENTRE RIGHT: After: When All is Revealed.

THIRD LEFT: Long term view.

BELOW: Born in Barnstaple, musical comedy artist Harry Welchman caused many a heart to flutter performing in *The Lady of the Rose* and *The Desert Song.* He made his screen debut in *The Maid of the Mountains* in 1932, a BIP picture directed by Lupino Lane.

BOTTOM LEFT: A scene from *The Maid of the Mountains* with Garry Marsh (l.), Nancy Brown and Harry Welchman.

BOTTOM RIGHT: Dennis Neilson-Terry and Anne Grey in Julius Hagen's *Murder at Covent Garden*, directed in 1932 by Leslie Hiscott.

TOP: The biggest break-through for British films in terms of world market competition and American box-office success was in 1933 with Alexander Korda's *The Private Life of Henry VIII* directed and produced by him for his London Film Productions which he had formed in 1931. Here, Henry (Charles Laughton) enjoys a wager with his fifth queen, Katherine Howard (Binnie Barnes).

CENTRE LEFT: Actor/comic/director and favourite of the 30s, Lupino Lane is seen here with Amy Veness in *A Southern Maid*, directed by Harry Hughes for BIP in 1933.

CENTRE RIGHT: Banqueting scene from *The Private Life of Henry VIII*. Young Thomas Culpepper (Robert Donat), standing behind the king, tries in vain to disguise his love for the queen, a digression that eventually leads to her execution. Stills by courtesy of London Film Productions Ltd.

BOTTOM LEFT: A case of *No Funny Business* for Jill Esmond and Laurence Olivier who married in 1930

and appeared in this 1933 John Stafford production directed by him and Victor Hanbury.

BOTTOM RIGHT: Born in 1907, Jessie Matthews made her theatrical debut in the revue *The Music Box* and stage success followed. Her early film appearances gave cause for anxiety and she still had the real break-through of *Evergreen* to come when she made this version of J. B. Priestley's novel *The Good Companions*, directed by Victor Saville in 1933 for Gaumont-Welsh-Pearson. Also appearing was another great star of the future, John Gielgud.

TOP LEFT: Max Miller, the 'Cheeky Chappie', born in 1895. Originally a variety hall comedian, his blue jokes and suggestive humour were considerably toned down for the cinema. He is seen here in *Friday the Thirteenth*, a Gainsborough picture produced by Michael Balcon and directed by Victor Saville in 1933.

TOP RIGHT: Frank Lawton and Belle Chrystal in *Friday the Thirteenth*.

ABOVE: A delightful still of Evelyn Laye in *Waltz Time* (1933). A much loved musical comedy star for more than two decades, she married leading man Frank Lawton. This film is based on Strauss's opera *Die Fledermaus*, produced for Gaumont by Herman Fellner and directed by William Thiele.

SECOND LEFT: D. A. Clarke-Smith and Gina Malo in a scene from *Waltz Time*.

THIRD LEFT: A Michael Balcon production for Gaumont of *Orders is Orders*, directed in 1933 by Walter Forde with Jane Carr and Ray Milland.

BOTTOM LEFT AND RIGHT: Comedian Gene Gerrard also had a good line in romantic patter and was very popular with the fair sex, qualities admirably demonstrated in these two stills from *Leave It To Me*, a 1933 BIP film directed by Monty Banks and also starring Molly Lamont.

TOP LEFT AND RIGHT: Kathleen Harrison (l.), Jessie Matthews and the village float in *The Man from Toronto*, the story of a widow posing as a maid in order to test the qualities of the man she must marry to inherit a fortune. A Michael Balcon production, directed by Sinclair Hill in 1933.

CENTRE LEFT: *Letting in the Sunshine*. Front line-up (l. to r.) Henry Mollison, Renee Gadd, Tonie Edgar Bruce and Mollie Lamont.

INSET: North country comic Albert Burden appeared in a number of comedies in the 30s, including *The Maid of the Mountains*, *It's a Boy*, *The Luck of the Navy* and (here) *Letting in the Sunshine*, directed for BIP by Lupino Lane in 1933.

BOTTOM: Jacket off and blowing his own trombone by directing himself and the cast in BIP's 1933 release *You Made Me Love You* is Monty Banks.

TOP LEFT: Touching performances from Minnie Rayner and Eliot Makeham in *I Lived with You*, directed by Maurice Elvey for Julius Hagen at Twickenham, 1933.

CENTRE LEFT: Ivor Novello starred in the screen adaptation of his own play *I Lived with You*, the story of an exiled Russian prince who is befriended by a shop assistant and her English suburban family and the effect that his stay has upon them. (L. to r.) Minnie Rayner, Jack Hawkins, Douglas Beaumont, Ivor Novello, Eliot Makeham, Ursula Jeans and Ida Lupino.

TOP RIGHT: Ever popular British star Anna Neagle whose films in the 30s included *Nell Gwyn, The Little Damozel, Peg of Old Drury, London Melody, Victoria the Great* and *Sixty Glorious Years*. She is seen here in *Bitter Sweet*, based on Noel Coward's operetta and produced and directed in 1933 by Herbert Wilcox with Freddie Young on camera.

BELOW AND RIGHT: Edmund Gwenn and Madeleine Carroll starred in *I Was a Spy*, a Gaumont-British Picture produced at Shepherd's Bush Studios in 1933 by Michael Balcon and directed by Victor Saville. The action takes place in Belgium and is based on a true story.

TOP LEFT: Turning the tables and cameras on to their director Monty Banks on the set of *Heads We Go* are (l. to r.) Constance Cummings, Fred Duprez and Claude Hulbert in this BIP production of 1933.

TOP RIGHT: Toasting another feather in their caps are Binnie Barnes (l.) and Constance Cummings in *Heads We Go*.

BOTTOM: **They Don't Make Films Like That Any More, Part III**
Blockbuster of 1934 was BIP's *Blossom Time*, based on the life of Schubert. Produced by Walter Mycroft and directed by Paul Stein, it starred Richard Tauber and, seen here being married in true *Sound of Music* style, Jane Baxter and Carl Esmond. Tauber sang an aria in the church accompanied by a choir relayed from another location.

TOP LEFT: *Contact* was a documentary film financed by Imperial Airways and Shell-Mex, made by the documentary film-maker Paul Rotha in 1933. It described the airline and its organisation.

TOP RIGHT: Following the success of *The Private Life of Henry VIII*, Korda continued his programme of visually ambitious and star-studded films with *The Scarlet Pimpernel* and (here) *Catherine the Great*. Douglas Fairbanks Junior as Grand Duke Peter encounters Flora Robson as the Empress Elizabeth at the Russian Imperial Court. Paul Czinner directed in 1934. Still by courtesy of London Film Productions Ltd.

ABOVE: David Manners and Greta Nissen in BIP's *The Luck of a Sailor*, directed in 1934 by Robert Milton.

CENTRE AND BOTTOM: Scenes from *Those were the Days*, a 1934 BIP production directed by Thomas Bentley, and starring (l.) Claude Allister, Iris Hoey, George Graves, Angela Baddeley and (r.) Will Hay, John Mills and H. F. Maltby.

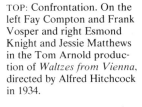

CENTRE LEFT AND RIGHT: Before and after treatment in *Doctor's Orders*, directed by Norman Lee for BIP in 1934, with Leslie Fuller.

BOTTOM LEFT: Baroness Orczy's historical adventure of the English aristocrat Sir Percy Blakeney whose foppish behaviour effectively disguises the real purpose of his activities (rescuing many victims of the French revolution) gave Leslie Howard a marvellous opportunity in 1934. He is seen here with Merle Oberon — later Mrs Alexander Korda — as his doubt-torn wife Marguerite. Produced for London Films by Alexander Korda and directed by Harold Young, *The Scarlet Pimpernel* also starred Raymond Massey as Chauvelin. Still by courtesy of London Film Productions Ltd.

BOTTOM RIGHT: Conrad Veidt and Benita Hume in *Jew Suss*, produced by Michael Balcon and directed by Lothar Mendes in 1934.

TOP LEFT AND RIGHT: Shades of *Victor/Victoria* to be made many years later with Julie Andrews as its star, *Girls will be Boys* was a BIP picture of 1934 directed by Marcel Varnel with Esmond Knight and Dolly Haas in the leads.

ABOVE: Also appearing in *Girls will be Boys* was 'grande dame' of the theatre, Irene Vanbrugh. Born in 1872 she appeared in a number of films including *Catherine the Great, Escape Me Never* and *Knight without Armour.*

SECOND LEFT: Rumour has it that there is a room in the 'Langham' — a former hotel opposite, and now owned by, the BBC — that is haunted and shunned by anyone familiar with its history. Not, one would hope, a form of vengeance for *Death at Broadcasting House* (1934), starring Ian Hunter and Mary Newland, produced by Hugh Perceval and directed by Reginald Denham.

THIRD LEFT: **'Why do we always have to watch what he wants to see?'**
Not a likely situation in *Love at Second Sight* with (l. to r.) Joan Gardner, Claude Hulbert, Ralph Ince, Marian Marsh and Anthony Bushell in the 1934 Julius Haimann production directed by Paul Merzbach.

BOTTOM LEFT: Happy ending, 30s style for Marian Marsh in *Love at Second Sight.*

BOTTOM RIGHT: Gracie Fields in the 1933 Julius Hagen production of *This Week of Grace*, directed by Maurice Elvey.

TOP: A location shot from *Jack Ahoy*, which starred Jack Hulbert and Nancy O'Neil. This Michael Balcon production was directed in 1934 by Walter Forde.

INSET: Another maritime location for director Walter Forde, seen here at a Thames midnight party on board the *New Dagenham* in the 30s, bidding goodnight to his hostess, film star Anna Lee.

CENTRE LEFT: A 1934 Gainsborough musical from Islington Studios, *Princess Charming*, directed by Maurice Elvey and starring Evelyn Laye, Henry Wilcoxon and George Grossmith (on steps).

BOTTOM LEFT: Gracie Fields in the now famous singing scene from *Sing As We Go* in which, as an unemployed mill-girl, she leads the workers through to a successful, no-strike, new productivity deal. This story by J. B. Priestley was produced and directed by Basil Dean in 1934.

BOTTOM RIGHT: Foyer card for *The Man Who Knew Too Much*, a 1934 Gaumont-British picture directed by Alfred Hitchcock.

TOP LEFT: Looking as if he is about to be enlightened and *Give Her a Ring* in the process is Clifford Mollison with Wendy Barrie.

TOP RIGHT: This telephone exchange for *Give Her a Ring*, directed by Arthur Woods for BIP in 1934, was built with the co-operation of the GPO who also assisted in details of operating the switchboard.

SECOND RIGHT: Meanwhile, Zelma O'Neal (l.) daydreams that someone will *Give Her a Ring* while her colleague Nadine March appears rather more headstrong.

THIRD RIGHT: **Don't ring us . . .**
Olive Blakeney and Eric Rhodes in *Give Her a Ring*.

BOTTOM LEFT: Director Phil Rosen cast Anthony Bushell and Tamara Desni in this 1934 story of a British nobleman helped by a Russian singer to rescue his son from a Siberian prison. *Forbidden Territory* was produced by Richard Wainwright for Progress Pictures.

BOTTOM RIGHT: Patric Knowles and Margaret Lockwood in Walter Mycroft's 1935 production of *Honours Easy*, directed by Herbert Brenon. Greta Nissen also starred in this adaptation from the play by Roland Pertwee.

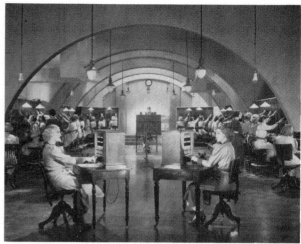

TOP: Alexander Korda directed and produced *The Private Life of Don Juan* in 1934 in which he again demonstrated his penchant for lavish sets and costumes. Still by courtesy of London Film Productions Ltd.

CENTRE LEFT: **'Sam, Sam, pick up thy musket . . .'** Pioneer Anson Dyer produced the cartoon *Sam and his Musket* in 1935. The famous monologue on which this film is based will always be associated with Stanley Holloway.

BOTTOM LEFT: (L. to r.) Henry Mollison, W. H. Berry, Zelma O'Neal, Finlay Currie and Lorna Storm in BIP's *Mister Cinders* directed in 1934 by Fred Zelnik.

BOTTOM RIGHT: Jessie Matthews's most famous musical and film was undoubtedly *Evergreen*, produced in 1934 by Michael Balcon and directed by Victor Saville. A delightful musical comedy, and a dual role performance from this doe-eyed actress in such numbers as 'Over My Shoulder' and 'Dancing on the Ceiling' will long be remembered by film buffs. (L. to r.) Betty Balfour, Patrick Ludlow, Jessie Matthews.

Mimi

The 1935 BIP feature directed by Paul Stein, celebrated the off-screen romance between Gertrude Lawrence and Douglas Fairbanks Junior (top). It also starred Diana Napier and Austin Trevor and featured beautifully designed sets and costumes. Understandably, critics have argued and will continue to argue the toss as to the desirability of casting the comic Miss Lawrence in the role of the dying consumptive, along with a script that added up to four writers getting it wrong. But if the critics did not like it, the audiences did, and that, after all, is what entertainment is really about.

CENTRE: Arriving for a little revelry are (l. to r.) Martin Walker, Harold Warrender, Carol Goodner, Douglas Fairbanks Junior, Gertrude Lawrence and Richard Bird.

BOTTOM LEFT: Gertie Lawrence craves the indulgence of Austin Trevor.

BOTTOM RIGHT: A little cheering up for Gertie Lawrence from Richard Bird and Carol Goodner.

Theatrical costumiers, Nathans founded in 1790, B. J. Simmons founded in 1860 and Berman's dating back to 1884 came together to supply many of the film costumes produced over the decades including those for *Mimi* and *Abdul the Damned* in 1935. Here, Diana Napier (main picture), Gertie Lawrence (above) and Carol Goodner (inset) model some of the *Mimi* gowns for the stills photographer.

ABOVE: British leading man of the day John Stuart with Adrienne Ames in a scene from *Abdul the Damned*. Produced by Max Schach for BIP-Capitol by Karl Grune in 1935.

TOP: Set and costumes from *Abdul the Damned* (1935).

CENTRE LEFT: A kneeling Lesley Wareing is unaware of the glances exchanged between Gladys Cooper and George Arliss (r.) in *The Iron Duke*.

BOTTOM LEFT: Leading costumiers Morris Angel supplied costumes for *The Iron Duke*, as played by distinguished stage actor George Arliss in this 1935 Gaumont British release directed by Victor Saville and produced by Michael Balcon.

BOTTOM RIGHT: Born in 1883, Tom Walls made his first stage appearance in 1905, then became actor/manager, leading up to producer of the long-running and widely popular Aldwych Farces. A number of these were transferred to the screen, including *Rookery Nook*, *Cuckoo in the Nest* and *Pot Luck*. This portrait of Walls is from *Me and Marlborough*, a comedy set in Flanders in the early 18th century, and directed for Gaumont by Victor Saville in 1935. Also starring were Cicely Courtneidge and Alfred Drayton.

TOP LEFT: If you want to get ahead get a hat . . . Hughie Green seems to be doing just that in Carol Reed's first film *Midshipman Easy*, produced for ATP by Basil Dean and Thorold Dickinson in 1935. (L. to r.) Esmee Church, Margaret Lockwood, Robert Adams, Arnold Lucy and Hughie Green.

TOP CENTRE:
Higher please. . . .
Deciding that he would not give two pins for another agent's chances, Eliot Makeham decides in favour of his new client (Enid Stamp-Taylor) in *Two Hearts in Harmony* produced for Time Pictures by John Clein and directed in 1935 by William Beaudine.

ABOVE: Leonora Corbett acquired her acting experience at Cambridge and on tour before her screen debut in 1932 in *Love on Wheels*. Seen here in *Heart's Desire*, an operatic love-story set in Vienna and starring Richard Tauber and Diana Napier.

CENTRE: Richard Tauber and Diana Napier on stage in *Heart's Desire*, a 1935 BIP release directed by Paul Stein.

BOTTOM LEFT: A link-scene from *Royal Cavalcade*, the film celebrating the Silver Jubilee of George V in 1935, a BIP presentation with episodes directed by Herbert Brenon, Thomas Bentley, Norman Lee, Walter Summers, Will Kellino and Marcel Varnel.

BOTTOM RIGHT: Patric Knowles and Grete Natzler in *The Student's Romance*, a 1935 Walter Mycroft production directed by Otto Kanturek.

TOP LEFT: Athene Seyler starred as Elizabeth I in *Drake of England* with Henry Mollison as John Doughty and Ben Webster (standing r.) as Lord Burghley.

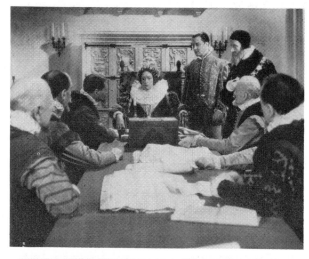

CENTRE LEFT: Matheson Lang in the name part kneels to Queen Elizabeth (Athene Seyler) in BIP's *Drake of England* directed by Arthur Woods in 1935.

TOP RIGHT: Ben Webster as Lord Burghley in *Drake of England*.

BOTTOM: Alfred Hitchcock was to delight film fans of 1935 with John Buchan's adventure *The Thirty-Nine Steps*, produced by Ivor Montagu for Gaumont British, starring Madeleine Carroll and Robert Donat.

TOP LEFT: An attractive study of Iris Ashley in the role of Margot in the 1935 BIP feature *I Give My Heart*, based on the opera *The Dubarry*, the story of a French milliner who weds a count in order to become a king's mistress. It was produced by Walter Mycroft and directed by Marcel Varnel.

TOP RIGHT: Margaret Bannerman as the Maréchale and Arthur Margetson as Count Dubarry in a scene from *I Give My Heart*.

CENTRE RIGHT: *Turn of the Tide* (1935), produced for British National by John Corfield and directed by Norman Walker. This simple but effective drama of two feuding fishing families brought together by a love match also turned the tide of J. Arthur Rank's film-making intentions. Unable to find distributors for his films, this brilliant businessman set up his own distribution and production company which mushroomed into the vast empire he controlled in later years. Here Niall McGinnis comes a-courting Geraldine Fitzgerald while Joan Maude plays chaperone.

BOTTOM: (L. to r.) Moore Marriott, Wilfrid Lawson, Niall McGinnis, Sam Livesey and John Garrick in *Turn of the Tide*.

TOP: *The Tunnel*, directed by Maurice Elvey in 1935 and produced for Gaumont-British by Michael Balcon. Elvey's career spanned four decades during which he made over 300 films. This film, his second science-fiction feature, concerned the building of an undersea tunnel between England and America in order to preserve peaceful relations, and did much to enhance his reputation.

CENTRE LEFT: *The Tunnel*: (l. to r.) Alan Jeayes, Helen Hayes, Percy Parsons, Madge Evans, Leslie Banks, Helen Vinson, Henry Oscar, Basil Sydney, C. Aubrey Smith.

BOTTOM LEFT: Arthur Margetson and Shirley Grey in *The Mystery of the Marie Celeste* directed in 1935 by Denison Clift and produced by H. Fraser Passmore for Hammer. Will Hammer had been a producer of summer shows and revues and began making films in the 30s. It was not however until after his re-entry into the industry following World War II, that the House of Hammer achieved international recognition.

BOTTOM RIGHT: Jessie Matthews in the famous cat-suit in Gaumont's lavish musical *It's Love Again*, produced by Michael Balcon and directed by Victor Saville in 1936.

ABOVE: J. Arthur Rank with David Lean.

TOP: **Pinewood Studios**
Born in 1888 and a major force in the history of British film making, magnate J. Arthur Rank entered the film industry in the 30s in partnership with Lady Yule and British National Films with the intention of making only films with a religious or strong moral theme. Unable to find a satisfactory release circuit for these films, he formed General Film Distributors with C. M. Woolf and acquired a part-Victorian mansion in Buckinghamshire in 1935, which he transformed into one of the finest studios in England. Pinewood Studios were officially opened in September 1936 and nearly 50 years on (headed by Cyril Howard who entered the industry in 1942) — the studios are renowned for dedication and expertise and continue to produce films for international markets.

BOTTOM: Anna Neagle in *London Melody* (1937). Elstree's loss and Pinewood's gain came in the shape of a fire that gutted Herbert Wilcox's British and Dominions Elstree Studios in February 1936. Rank welcomed the injection of fresh capital from Wilcox's insurance which gave him part-ownership of Pinewood. Ironically the first sequences to be shot at the new studios were for the completion of the Wilcox production *London Melody* which had been started at Elstree.

TOP LEFT: Marcel Hellman co-produced *The Amateur Gentleman* with Douglas Fairbanks Junior who also starred in the film directed by Thornton Freeland in 1936. On either side are Gunner Moire (l.) and Gordon Harker. The story is of an innkeeper's son posing as an aristocrat in order to prove that his father is innocent of theft.

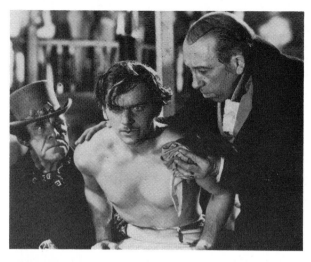

TOP RIGHT: Thanks to the reputation earned for *The Private Life of Henry VIII* and his success with *The Scarlet Pimpernel*, financial backing was given by the Prudential Insurance Company which enabled Alexander Korda to build Denham Studios, officially opened in 1936.

CENTRE LEFT AND RIGHT: The first major feature for Korda's London Film Productions at Denham — considered by many to be one of his finest achievements — was *Rembrandt*, produced and directed by Korda in 1936. It starred Charles Laughton in the title role and Gertrude Lawrence as his housekeeper. Korda's incredible eye for detail, Vincent Korda's sets, beautifully photographed by Georges Perinal earmarked this film as one of the real classics of the 30s. Stills by courtesy of London Film Productions Ltd.

BOTTOM:
Korda and friends, 1936
Alexander Korda (top left) with Douglas Fairbanks Junior, Richard Tauber, Diana Napier, Alan Hale; (Second row) Flora Robson, Elsa Lanchester, Marlene Dietrich, Tamara Desni, Elizabeth Bergner, William K. Conrad, Erich Pommer, Murray Silverstone; (Front) Conrad Veidt, Victor Saville (on floor), Ann Harding, Marie Tempest, Renee Ray, Edward G. Robinson, Googie Withers.

TOP LEFT: (L. to r.) Hazel Terry, Hugh Sinclair, and Nils Asther in *The Marriage of Corbal*. This tale of adventure during the French Revolution was produced by Max Schach and directed for Capitol by Karl Grune in 1936.

TOP RIGHT: A major documentary in the 30s produced for the GPO film unit by Basil Wright and Harry Watt was *Nightmail* (1936), which included as narrative a poem by W. H. Auden. The film shows in fine, dramatic detail the mail train's journey from London to Glasgow.

CENTRE LEFT: Jean Parker and Robert Donat in *The Ghost Goes West*, directed by Rene Clair for Korda in 1936. Donat played the dual role of the ghost and his descendant, whose castle is transported to Florida by an American millionaire. Still by courtesy of London Film Productions Ltd.

CENTRE RIGHT: Aileen Marson and Francis Lister in *Living Dangerously*, a 1936 BIP production directed by Herbert Brenon.

BOTTOM: A bevy of beauties from *The Man who could Work Miracles*, directed by Lothar Mendes for Korda in 1936 and based on a short story by H. G. Wells.

ABOVE: Morton Selten in *Fire Over England*, produced by Erich Pommer and directed by William K. Howard in 1936. Born in 1860, Selten achieved West End stage success before appearing in such films as *Service for Ladies, Wedding Rehearsal* and *The Shadow Between*.

RIGHT: Romantic pair Vivien Leigh and Laurence Olivier in *Fire Over England* — they were to marry in 1940.

TOP LEFT: Leslie Banks, English actor born in 1890. His first important film role was in America in *The Most Dangerous Game*. His British films included *The Tunnel*, *Fire over England* and *Jamaica Inn*.

TOP RIGHT: Betty Ann Davies and comedian Claude Dampier in *She Knew What She Wanted*, produced and directed by Thomas Bentley in 1936.

CENTRE RIGHT: Fred Conyngham (l.), Betty Ann Davies and Albert Burdon in *She Knew What She Wanted*.

BOTTOM: *Things to Come* 1936.

BELOW: With a film score by Sir Arthur Bliss and a fine cast headed by Raymond Massey, Alexander Korda's production of *Things to Come* was an impressive artistic achievement. Based on H. G. Wells's futuristic novel in which scientists attempt to rebuild a war-torn Earth, the film was directed by William Cameron Menzies. Many of the film's special effects were made at Worton Hall Studios, Isleworth.

TOP LEFT: Nova Pilbeam as the ill-fated Lady Jane Grey with John Mills as Lord Guildford in *Tudor Rose*, a Gainsborough production directed by Robert Stevenson in 1936.

SECOND LEFT: *The Secret Agent*: Peter Lorre (l.), John Gielgud and Madeleine Carroll appeared in this 1936 thriller directed by Alfred Hitchcock and produced for Gaumont-British by Ivor Montagu.

TOP RIGHT: Popular revue artist, often teamed with Jack Buchanan, Elsie Randolph appeared in *This'll Make You Whistle* produced and directed in 1936 by Herbert Wilcox. Also starring were Jack Buchanan, William Kendall and Jean Gillie.

BOTTOM AND BELOW: Scenes from *Good Morning Boys*, Will Hay's fourth comedy for Gainsborough, produced by Edward Black and directed by Marcel Varnel in 1937. The cast included Martita Hunt, Peter Gawthorne and Charles Hawtrey.

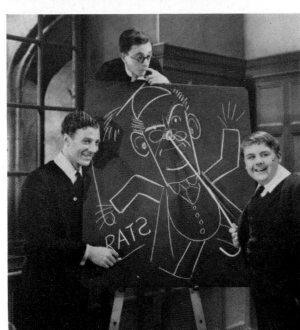

ABOVE: Malcolm Keen. Brilliant stage actor and manager of the Lyric Theatre in the late 20s, he appeared in the films *The Skin Game. Wolves, The Manxman. Jealousy.*

TOP LEFT: Merle Oberon and Laurence Olivier in *The Divorce of Lady X*, the story of a barrister being pursued by a titled lady posing as a divorce client. Tim Whelan directed this Alexander Korda production in 1937. Still by courtesy of London Film Productions Ltd.

TOP RIGHT: Anna Neagle starred in Herbert Wilcox's *Victoria the Great* (1937), based on the play *Victoria Regina* by Laurence Housman.

CENTRE LEFT: It looks like a case of the little woman giving way yet again . . . Phillips Holmes and Diana Churchill in BIP's 1937 feature *The Dominant Sex*, directed by Herbert Brenon.

BOTTOM: Fair cop . . . Richard Murdoch (l.) trips the light fantastic with Syd Walker in *Over She Goes*, an ABPC production directed by Graham Cutts in 1937.

The delightful comedienne Cicely Courtneidge began her stage career in 1901. With her comedy star husband Jack Hulbert, she appeared in a number of films including *Take my Tip* which was directed for Gaumont-British in 1937 by Herbert Mason.

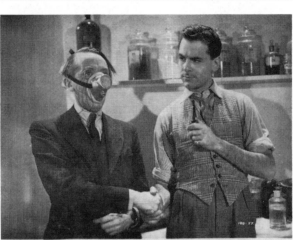

TOP LEFT: Could it be that Henry Wilcoxon, held here by John Laurie, has met his just deserts at the hands of Paul Robeson (r.)? *Jericho* (1937) was a Buckingham production by Walter Futter and Max Schach; direction by Thornton Freeland.

TOP RIGHT: Will Fyffe (c.) does not seem to fancy his chances with Maire O'Neill and Frank Pettingell in *Spring Handicap*, the story of a wife determined to prevent her husband frittering away a legacy, directed for ABPC by Herbert Brenon in 1937.

CENTRE LEFT: Trefor Jones and Mary Ellis in the ABPC screen adaptation of one of Ivor Novello's most popular plays, *Glamorous Night*, directed by Brian Desmond Hurst in 1937.

CENTRE RIGHT: *Goodbye and good luck . . .* Claud Allister (l.) as Algy Longworth decides the whole thing's a gas. Bulldog Drummond, played by heartthrob John Lodge, seems less sure. An ABPC film directed in 1937 by Norman Lee.

BOTTOM LEFT: *Love From a Stranger*: (L. to r.) Binnie Hale, Basil Rathbone and Ann Harding starred in this Agatha Christie thriller produced for Trafalgar by Max Schach and directed in 1937 by Rowland V. Lee.

BOTTOM RIGHT: Alexander Korda paid nearly half a million dollars for the services of Marlene Dietrich to star opposite Robert Donat in *A Knight without Armour*, set in revolutionary Russia. Directed by Jacques Feyder in 1937. Still by courtesy of London Film Productions Ltd.

TOP LEFT: Will Hay looks prepared to forego the kipper dressing as offered by Graham Moffatt while Moore Marriott ponders over the situation in this classic Marcel Varnel comedy *Oh. Mr Porter!* Produced in 1937 by Edward Black for Gainsborough.

TOP RIGHT: **Mother!**
A touch of *The Terror* for Linden Travers and Bernard Lee in the ABPC version of Edgar Wallace's thriller, directed by Richard Bird in 1937.

CENTRE LEFT: 'Usual retouching on both' is a direction for the stills man — not for the dentist. Robertson Hare with patient Ellen Pollock in *Aren't Men Beasts?*, produced by Walter Mycroft and directed by Graham Cutts in 1937.

SECOND RIGHT: (L. to r.) Alfred Drayton, Billy Milton, and Robertson Hare in *Aren't Men Beasts?*

BOTTOM LEFT: Publicity still of Eve Gray in *The Vicar of Bray*.

THIRD RIGHT: An unusually serious Stanley Holloway in *The Vicar of Bray*, seen here with Hamilton Price. Directed by Henry Edwards in 1937 for J. H. Productions.

BOTTOM RIGHT: Poster for *Marigold*, produced by ABPC in 1938 and directed by Thomas Bentley.

It just goes to show what a little pampering can do for a girl. Diana Churchill and Peter Murray Hill provide the full commercial in *Jane Steps Out*, produced for ABPC by Walter Mycroft and directed by Paul Stein in 1938.

TOP LEFT: Vivacious Pat Kirkwood and Dave Willis in *Save a Little Sunshine*, produced by Warwick Ward and directed by Norman Lee in 1938.

CENTRE LEFT: Two outstanding British comics, Tommy Trinder (l.) and Max Wall in *Save a Little Sunshine*.

TOP RIGHT: *Vessel of Wrath* (1938) seems to catch the mood of Elsa Lanchester, heartily reciprocated by Charles Laughton in the Mayflower production by Erich Pommer of a story by W. Somerset Maugham. Directed by Pommer, it also starred Robert Newton and Tyrone Guthrie.

BOTTOM LEFT: Ladies of the 30s reached for their Cologne on seeing screen heroes such as Otto Kruger (l.) and John Clements in *Star of the Circus*. Produced by Walter Mycroft in 1938 and directed by Albert de Courville. The lady in the American football ensemble is Gertrude Michael.

BOTTOM RIGHT: In view of his memorable performance as the professor of phonetics who transforms a cockney flower girl into a lady, it is surprising that Leslie Howard was not Shaw's first choice for the role. Here, Henry Higgins encounters his pupil (Wendy Hiller). Produced by Gabriel Pascal and directed by Anthony Asquith and Leslie Howard, *Pygmalion* was one of the top moneymakers of 1939.

TOP: Anna Neagle and Herbert Wilcox with Stephen Watts of the *Express*, filming at Buckingham Palace in 1938 for Wilcox's *Sixty Glorious Years*. Actual 'Windsor Greys' seen in the background were used in the film at the request of King George VI.

BOTTOM LEFT: Even with egg and chips at 5d (less than 3 new pence), life still seems hard for Gus McNaughton talking to Doctor Robert Donat in *The Citadel*, the MGM-British adaptation of A. J. Cronin's novel produced by Victor Saville and directed by King Vidor in 1938.

BOTTOM RIGHT: *Yes, Madam?* starred Diana Churchill and Bobby Howes. A 1938 ABPC production directed by Norman Lee.

TOP LEFT: Alexander Korda misjudged the mood of the Empire film market when he produced *The Drum* (1938), directed by his brother, Zoltan Korda. Although popular in the UK, the film about an Indian prince who is helped to thwart a frontier rising by one Captain Carruthers and company, was banned in India.

TOP RIGHT: (L. to r.) Raymond Massey, David Tree, Roger Livesey, Valerie Hobson, Archibald Batty, Frederick Culley in *The Drum*, which also starred Desmond Tester and Sabu.

CENTRE: Huggett fore-runners all set for the *Bank Holiday*. Wally Patch and Kathleen Harrison, seen here with their screen family, played the struggling parents in this 1938 Gainsborough production directed by Carol Reed. Also in the film were John Lodge, Margaret Lockwood, Wilfred Lawson, Hugh Williams and Rene Ray.

BOTTOM LEFT: **Aimez-vous maracas?** John Lodge and Gertrude Michael in ABPC's *Just Like a Woman*, directed by Paul Stein in 1938.

BOTTOM RIGHT: Judy Kelly and Clifford Evans in *Luck of the Navy*, produced by Walter Mycroft and directed by Norman Lee in 1938.

MARGARET LOCKWOOD ~ KATHLEEN HARRISON ~ JOHN LODGE in
BANK HOLIDAY Cert. A with HUGH WILLIAMS
A GAINSBOROUGH PICTURE Released by G.F.D.

A marvellous cast directed by Alfred Hitchcock, a script by Sidney Gilliat and Frank Launder, plus Basil Radford and Naunton Wayne more interested in the test score than intrigue was the recipe for *The Lady Vanishes*, the very successful Gainsborough comedy thriller in 1938. LEFT: (L. to r.) Naunton Wayne, Margaret Lockwood, Dame May Whitty, Michael Redgrave, Basil Radford and Cecil Parker, and RIGHT: (L. to r.) Googie Withers, Margaret Lockwood and Sally Stewart.

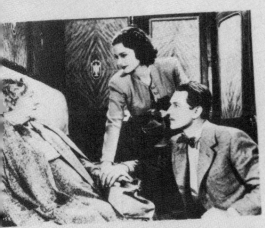

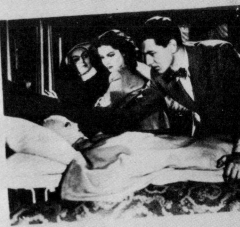

MARGARET LOCKWOOD
MICHAEL REDGRAVE
PAUL LUKAS · DAME MAY WHITTY
in
"The LADY VANISHES"
with
Cecil Parker · Linden Travers · Mary Clare
Based on the story "The Wheel Spins" by Ethel Lina White
Directed by ALFRED HITCHCOCK
"A" Censor Certificate
A GAINSBOROUGH PICTURE
Distributed by Metro-Goldwyn-Mayer Pictures ltd

TOP LEFT: Fresh from their success at the Palladium, the Crazy Gang decided to invade the cinema with their mad humour. *Alf's Button Afloat*, produced by Edward Black and directed by Marcel Varnel in 1938, was one of the four films they made for Gainsborough; it would probably be true to say that the studios were never the same again. Here the Gang (l. to r.) Teddy Knox, Jimmy Nervo, Charlie Naughton, Chesney Allen, Bud Flanagan, and Jimmy Gold liven up the old fairy tale Aladdin with a button instead of a lamp while Alastair Sim as the genie in need of a manicure, contributes his own zany blend of magic.

TOP RIGHT: The two girls with a crush on *The Housemaster* (Otto Kruger) are Renee Ray (l.) and Diana Churchill. Directed by Herbert Brenon in 1938 for ABPC.

CENTRE LEFT: 'Charles and Troupe' perform to the queues outside the Holborn Empire. (L. to r.) Charles Laughton (who had to learn to sing, dance and play the tin whistle), Tyrone Guthrie, Gus McNaughton and Vivien Leigh in *St Martin's Lane*, an Erich Pommer production directed by Tim Whelan, 1938.

SECOND RIGHT: Vivien Leigh and Rex Harrison in *St Martin's Lane*.

BOTTOM LEFT: *Come on George* seems to be the advice given by Pat Kirkwood to Lancashire comedian George Formby in Jack Kitchin's production of 1939, directed by Anthony Kimmins.

THIRD RIGHT: Googie Withers, Edward Everett Horton and Jack Buchanan in *The Gang's All Here*, directed by Thornton Freeland for ABPC in 1939.

BOTTOM RIGHT: Flora Robson (l.) with Ann Todd on location for *Poison Pen*, a 1939 ABPC drama concerning a vicar's spinster sister and her vitriolic writings. Directed by Paul Stein.

TOP: Lobby card for the MGM-British production *Goodbye Mr Chips* (1939) for which Robert Donat won an Oscar in the role of the schoolmaster, a touching character from the novel by James Hilton. The film also starred Greer Garson, Paul Henreid and John Mills and was directed by Sam Wood.

BOTTOM LEFT: Knock-out child actor destined for a long and successful acting career, Roddy McDowell in the 1939 ABPC production of the very popular *Just William*, directed by Graham Cutts.

CENTRE RIGHT: Naval manoeuvres: Greta Gynt and Jack Buchanan in *The Middle Watch* directed by Thomas Bentley for ABPC in 1939.

BOTTOM RIGHT: Portly comedian Fred Emney gets advice and consternation from Romney Brent (l.) and Jack Buchanan.

TOP LEFT: Terence Rattigan's comedy *French Without Tears* provided a splendid vehicle for Guy Middleton, Ellen Drew and Ray Milland in the Two Cities production of 1939, directed by Anthony Asquith.

TOP RIGHT: Director Walter Forde greets Pamela Ostrer who became Pamela Kellino who became Mrs James Mason.

BELOW: With many studios closing at the outbreak of war, the title song from *The Lambeth Walk*, produced by Anthony Havelock-Allan and directed by Albert de Courville in 1939, will remain in the minds of many as a memory of a dying era.

Lupino Lane

"The LAMBETH WALK"

with

SEYMOUR HICKS · SALLY GRAY

A Pinebrook Production distributed by Metro-Goldwyn-Mayer Ltd.

Ralph Richardson (l.) and Donald Gray in A. E. W. Mason's *The Four Feathers* brought to the screen in 1939 by Alexander Korda and Irving Asher. Also starring were John Clements and C. Aubrey Smith, and Zoltan Korda directed. Still by courtesy of London Film Productions Ltd.

TOP: Atmospheric still and set from *Jamaica Inn* with cloak and gun smoothie Laughton threatening the lovely Maureen O'Hara.

BOTTOM: Emlyn Williams prepares the rope, Leslie Banks directs operations and Mervyn Johns prepares the victim Robert Newton in *Jamaica Inn*.

BELOW: A villainous Charles Laughton (l.), heroine Maureen O'Hara and Robert Newton totally heroic in Erich Pommer's 1939 screen adaptation of Daphne du Maurier's 18th century Cornish melodrama *Jamaica Inn*, directed by Alfred Hitchcock.

War and peace
1940-1949

THOUGHTS OF air-raid sirens, bombs and gas-masks did not deter the film fan from going to the pictures during the war years. On the contrary, the one thing that the public needed more than anything else during the blitz and the buzz-bombs was some sheer escapism — and they certainly flocked and queued to see their favourite stars and films.

The Government requisitioned some studios at the outbreak of war. Pinewood was used for food and grain storage, Shepperton was taken over by Vickers Aircraft, the Elstree studios of ABPC became a Royal Ordnance Corps depot and their film production was moved to Welwyn. The studios left to function — albeit under threat from the enemy and the Ministry of Defence (who were keen to keep storage and factory space free) — were Ealing, part of Denham, Hammersmith, Islington, Shepherd's Bush, Teddington and Welwyn. In spite of difficulties in obtaining supplies, technicians and artists, some marvellous films were produced.

From 1939 to 1945, films could be more or less divided into three categories. Full-length, direct propaganda films, made by loyal commercial companies in an effort to fly the flag and boost morale, which they undoubtedly did with films such as *The Way to the Stars, The Way Ahead, 49th Parallel, Target For Tonight, Millions Like Us* and *In Which We Serve*. The remarkable thing is that these were all good films, probably due to the fact that the highly dramatic situations being enacted were for real, bringing a sense of unity of purpose to the productions. Then there were instructional films made under Government or Service sponsorship, produced by Service Film Units or farmed out to commercial studios, and finally the non-propaganda, escapist film comedy or romance making the point for closely knit family circles and maintaining a high morale. *Sailors Three, The Man in Grey, Dear Octopus* and *This Happy Breed* were good examples of this type of production.

After the war, studios at Pinewood, Shepperton and those of ABPC at Elstree reopened and by 1949, the following studios were also in operation as well as a number of smaller ones: Amalgamated, Beaconsfield, British National, Bushey, Denham, Ealing, Gate, Highbury, Islington, Lime Grove, Marylebone, Merton Park, Nettlefold, Pathé, Riverside, Southall, Twickenham, Welwyn and Wembley.

The major force behind Ealing Studios' greatest triumphs — their renowned comedies during the 40s and 50s — was Michael Balcon. He entered the industry just after World War I and took over production at Gaumont-British in the early 30s. In 1938 he became head of production at Ealing and from then on the names of Balcon and Ealing were inextricably linked, resulting in such films as *The Proud Valley, My Learned Friend, Champagne Charlie, Dead of Night, Nicholas Nickleby, Whisky Galore, Saraband for Dead Lovers, Scott of the Antarctic* and *Kind Hearts and Coronets*, all made at Ealing during the 40s, along with many more.

The splendid films of Michael Powell and Emeric Pressburger also became box-office successes both during and after the war — films such as *A Matter of Life and Death, The Life and Death of Colonel Blimp, Black Narcissus* and *The Red Shoes*, made in their highly individual style. Popular Gainsborough melodramas including *Madonna of the Seven Moons, The Wicked Lady* and *Love Story* are perhaps some of the most nostalgia-evoking films of the decade. Thoughts of the Herbert Wilcox successes — *Piccadilly Incident, Spring in Park Lane, I Live in Grosvenor Square, The Courtneys of Curzon Street* — in which Anna Neagle was frequently partnered by Michael Wilding also conjure up many pleasant memories. Laurence Olivier's *Hamlet* and *Henry V*; David Lean's *Brief Encounter, Great Expectations* and *Oliver Twist*; Carol Reed's *Odd Man Out, The Fallen Idol* and *The Third Man*; Sydney Box's *The Seventh Veil* still rank as some of the finest films ever produced in Britain.

The reopening of the studios also presented an opportunity for many of the younger and lesser known actors who were eager to make their way in films. Richard Attenborough, Dirk Bogarde, Derek Bond, Michael Denison, Diana Dors, Bryan Forbes, Dulcie Gray, Joan Greenwood, Sally Ann Howes, Glynis Johns, Kenneth More, Lana Morris, Barbara Murray, Anthony Newley, Sheila Sim, Jean Simmons, Anthony Steel and David Tomlinson all came into their own from the mid-forties onwards.

In spite of the difficulties brought on by the war and the immediate post-war period, the industry had nevertheless been extremely active. Talk, however, was beginning to be heard in the Wardour Street corridors of power, about the rapidly growing television audiences. It was not very serious, though,

Making good propaganda and bringing much needed comic relief to war-torn Britain in 1940 were *Sailors Three*, (l. to r.) Michael Wilding, Tommy Trinder and Claude Hulbert, in a story about three inebriated gentlemen from the Senior Service who manage to board an enemy battleship and capture it. Michael Balcon had become head of production at Ealing Studios in 1938 and this film was one of the last to be directed by Walter Forde for the studio as the new regime got under way. The film certainly reflected Forde's earlier career as silent film comedian.

perhaps akin to the type of comment that had been levied at the possibility of sound in 1928/29.

There were, after all, only 40,000 television receivers in London in 1947 and it was hard to believe that this number would grow to such an extent as to deprive the cinema of its fans and potential patrons. Hardly even worth considering. As to the new quota system being talked about and something called the Eady Levy in 1949 — well, some people had nothing better to do than to go around scaremongering.

TOP LEFT: Elizabeth Allan and Alec Clunes in a garage love interlude from the film version of the stage success *Saloon Bar* which also starred Gordon Harker. It was produced by Culley Forde for Ealing Studios in 1940 and directed by Walter Forde.

TOP RIGHT: *Old Mother Riley in Society* (1940), produced by John Corfield for British National and directed by John Baxter. Arthur Lucan *was* Old Mother Riley, a conniving washerwoman with a shrill Irish accent and a long-suffering daughter, Kitty (played by his wife Kitty McShane). A much loved double act of film, radio and music-hall during the 30s and 40s.

CENTRE LEFT: Jack Hawkins and Phyllis Brooks in Edgar Wallace's *The Flying Squad*, a 1940 ABPC production directed by Herbert Brenon.

CENTRE RIGHT: 'She will eat oysters out of season . . .' In fact, the lady's indisposition is caused by fear of her husband's strange behaviour in *Gaslight*, a 1940 melodrama directed by Thorold Dickinson for British National. (L. to r.) Diana Wynyard, Anton Walbrook and Mary Hinton.

BOTTOM: A typical British cinema lobby card of 1940 advertising *Night Train to Munich*, a thriller that would have given enormous pleasure to crime and railway buffs alike. Produced by Edward Black, it was directed by Carol Reed.

TOP LEFT: Alfred Lord Tennyson's great-grandson, Pen Tennyson directed *The Proud Valley* for Ealing in 1940. A story of a Welsh mining community starring (l. to r.) Edward Chapman, Rachel Thomas and Paul Robeson.

TOP RIGHT: An ABPC 1940 publicity still for *Bulldog Sees it Through* with (l. to r.) Greta Gynt, Googie Withers, David Hutcheson and Jack Buchanan. Directed by Harold Huth.

OPPOSITE, BOTTOM: Lending an ear in Alexander Korda's magical 1940 production of *The Thief of Baghdad* was genie Rex Ingram. Although completed in the US, the film's very special effects originated at the Denham studios and were outstanding for their time. Directors of the film included Michael Powell, Ludwig Berger, and Tim Whelan. Still by courtesy of London Film Productions Ltd.

TOP LEFT: Wife-hunting Basil Sydney prepares for the chase in *The Farmer's Wife* the 1941 ABPC remake with Nora Swinburne and Wilfrid Lawson. Directed by Norman Lee and Leslie Arliss.

TOP RIGHT: Surrounded by an admiring audience, north country comedian George Formby gets to work on his famous ukulele in *Let George Do It*, produced for Ealing by Basil Dearden in 1940 and directed by Marcel Varnel.

BOTTOM: Phyllis Calvert and George Formby in *Let George Do It*.

O·F·I–123.

OPPOSITE: Top moneymaker of 1942, *49th Parallel*, not only had a star cast, but a formidable production team as well, including producer Michael Powell (seated) and (crouching by camera, spectacled) Freddie Young. Powell also directed this film from a screenplay by Emeric Pressburger and Rodney Ackland.

TOP RIGHT AND ABOVE: Before and after. Laurence Olivier in *49th Parallel*

CENTRE: Glynis Johns in *49th Parallel*

BOTTOM RIGHT: A thoughtful study of Leslie Howard in *49th Parallel*, the war-time adventure drama of a ruthless German U-boat commander attempting to rescue his stranded crew by conveying them across Canada into neutral America. The cast included Eric Portman as the chilling commander, Anton Walbrook and Raymond Massey.

TOP LEFT: Looking for the *Target for Tonight*, were the actual officers and crews of Bomber Command in this stirring wartime propaganda feature, made by Harry Watt in 1941. The story of a particular bomber crew making a routine raid on Germany, it was widely shown in America in the hope of rallying support for Britain's growing plight — which it did.

CENTRE LEFT: On a lighter note, Walter Mycroft cast (l. to r.) Basil Sydney, Michael Wilding and Enid Stamp-Taylor in *Spring Meeting* in 1941.

TOP RIGHT: Michael Wilding and Nova Pilbeam in *Spring Meeting*.

BOTTOM: (L. to r.) Rex Harrison, Sybil Thorndike, Wendy Hiller (hatless) watch Robert Morley write out a donation in Shaw's *Major Barbara*, an act that prompts her resignation from the Salvation Army. Penelope Dudley-Ward, Marie Lohr and Marie Ault also played in this Gabriel Pascal production which he also directed in 1941.

TOP LEFT: Singularly unimpressed by Leslie Howard's explanations as to how good will ultimately triumph over evil, Francis L. Sullivan prefers a physical show of strength to an aesthetic one in *Pimpernel Smith*, directed by Howard for British National in 1941.

TOP RIGHT: *This Man is Dangerous* seems an apt title for the John Argyle production of 1941 which starred Margaret Vyner and a very handsome James Mason who were directed by Lawrence Huntington.

CENTRE: As well as being remembered for the performances of Anton Walbrook and Sally Gray, *Dangerous Moonlight* will also bring to mind its wartime story and accompanying memories as imposed by the 'Warsaw Concerto' written by Richard Addinsell. Produced by William Sistrom, it was directed in 1941 by Brian Desmond Hurst.

BOTTOM LEFT: Complete with gasmask, Leslie Fuller seems intent on getting down all the details in *My Wife's Family*. (L. to r.) Wylie Watson, John Warwick, Leslie Fuller, Margaret Scudamore, Joan Greenwood and Patricia Roc. Produced and directed by Walter Mycroft for ABPC in 1941.

BOTTOM RIGHT: Michael Rennie (l.) and Wilfrid Lawson in *Tower of Terror*, a spy thriller set in a lighthouse. Directed by Lawrence Huntington in 1941 for ABPC.

TOP LEFT: Proving that *Women Aren't Angels*, because in this case they are men, are Alfred (knobbly knees) Drayton and Robertson Hare. Produced by former silent star Warwick Ward and directed by Lawrence Huntington in 1942.

TOP RIGHT: Gordon Jackson (c.), in his screen debut, clings to the spoils of war while comrade Tommy Trinder decides that the situation is less than sparkling when confronted by Clifford Evans in *The Foreman went to France*. From a storyline by J. B. Priestley, directed by Charles Frend for Ealing in 1942, produced by Alberto Cavalcanti.

In Which We Serve (1942). This much acclaimed box-office draw originated from Lord Louis Mountbatten who had recounted some of his own wartime experiences — including the sinking of his own ship — to Noel Coward. Coward obtained permission to base his story on these experiences, provided that no real names or characters were used. *In Which We Serve* was produced by Coward who also co-directed with David Lean, resulting in a beautifully acted and directed film. The cast included Noel Coward (bottom left), John Mills and Kathleen Harrison (bottom right), Richard Attenborough, Bernard Miles, Celia Johnson, Kay Walsh and many more. The film, described as 'one of the screen's proudest achievements at any time in any country', had immense propaganda value in America and gave a tremendous boost to public morale in Britain. It is also still quite capable of bringing a lump to an unsuspecting mature throat.

CENTRE: Praying for a miracle — a scene from *In Which We Serve.*

TOP LEFT: Daisy (Patricia Hayes) and Mrs Collins (Muriel George) register fear and uncertainty in *Went the Day Well?*, a wartime drama of an English village taken over by a platoon of Germans. Based on a Graham Greene story, it was directed by Cavalcanti for Michael Balcon in 1942.

TOP RIGHT: Bad timing for Claude Hulbert (l.) and Will Hay caught by an unbalanced Mervyn Johns in Big Ben's belfry in *My Learned Friend*, produced for Ealing by Robert Hamer and co-directed by Will Hay and Basil Dearden in 1943.

LONG PICTURE: Dying 'Spitfire' designer R. J. Mitchell (Leslie Howard) asks Crisp (David Niven) for news from the Air Ministry in *The First of the Few*, produced by Leslie Howard, Adrian Brunel, George King and John Stafford. Directed by Leslie Howard in 1942, who sadly died the following year when his plane was reported missing.

LEFT: (L. to r.) Eric Portman, Jack Watling and John Mills and (right and bottom left) other scenes from *We Dive At Dawn*. A Gainsborough picture directed by Anthony Asquith in 1943.

BOTTOM RIGHT: Continuing the theme of patriotism during the war years, Mary Morris, Michael Wilding and John Clements were cast in *Undercover*, a drama set in Yugoslavia, about a doctor posing as a collaborator in order to save a rebel family. Directed for Ealing by Sergei Nolbandov in 1943.

TOP LEFT: Roger Livesey and Deborah Kerr in the Powell-Pressburger production of *The Life and Death of Colonel Blimp* (1943). A film that was to do well at the box-office, but which received no bouquets from Winston Churchill or the War Office who felt that certain attitudes expressed in the film bordered on disloyalty to king and country.

CENTRE LEFT: *It's That Man Again* needs no introduction to wartime ITMA fans as — and in spite of the blackout — Tommy Handley gets lit up from 'Boss, something terrible has happened' Sidney Keith as Sam Scram.

TOP RIGHT: 'Can I do yer now, Sir?' was the ever-hopeful cry of Mrs Mop (Dorothy Summers), one of the stalwarts of the *It's That Man Again* radio show. This film version was produced by Edward Black for Gainsborough in 1943 and directed by Walter Forde.

BOTTOM: *Dear Octopus* was a Gainsborough favourite which brought together the talents of many popular artists. Produced by Edward Black and directed by Harold French in 1943, it told the story of a family's reunion at a golden wedding anniversary celebration and was an excellent vehicle for conveying the attitudes and behaviour of the so-called British middle and upper classes of the time. (L. to r.) back row Nora Swinburne, Michael Wilding, Margaret Lockwood, Basil Radford, Antoinette Cellier, Celia Johnson; front row: Athene Seyler, Frederick Leister, Helen Haye, Madge Compton and the children Ann Stephens and Derek Lansiaux.

TOP: With several studios commandeered by Whitehall for the duration of the war — Elstree and Pinewood, for example, were both used for military and storage purposes — Ealing and Gainsborough came to the fore in screen entertainment. Gainsborough were to promote a number of players to star status who were certainly as popular as their Hollywood counterparts. Amongst their number were Phyllis Calvert, James Mason, Margaret Lockwood, Stewart Granger and Patricia Roc. These films and their stars not only provided the public with much needed escapism from their worries, gasmasks and air-raid shelters, they also produced for the box-office a series of smash-hits, far more acceptable than the direct hits of the era. Here, James Mason — the man the ladies loved to hate — and Phyllis Calvert, usually the goodie, play a scene in *The Man in Grey*. The film also starred Margaret Lockwood as the baddie and Stewart Granger, as usual, played the hero. It was back to the style of early 20s all over again. The production for Gainsborough was by Edward Black and directed by Leslie Arliss in 1943.

BOTTOM: Scenes from *The Demi-Paradise*, directed by Anthony Asquith in 1943 and produced for Two Cities by Anatole de Grunwald. The cast included Penelope Dudley-Ward and Guy Middleton (centre left), Laurence Olivier and Margaret Rutherford (bottom left) and Joyce Grenfell (bottom right).

Millions Like Us was another film to touch the heart and nerve ends in 1943. A munitions factory formed the backcloth to this war drama, which starred Eric Portman, Anne Crawford, Patricia Roc, Basil Radford and Naunton Wayne, and gave a young actor, Gordon Jackson, the opportunity of turning in an excellent performance as a tongue-tied Scottish airman in love for the first time. This was also the first feature as writer/directors for Frank Launder and Sidney Gilliat. An Edward Black production for Gainsborough.

TOP LEFT: Old and new stars of the decade combine to give this still from *The Came to a City* a special quality. It was directed by Basil Dearden for Ealing in 1944. (L. to r.) Ada Reeve, Renee Gadd, John Clements, Googie Withers, Frances Rowe, Raymond Huntley, Norman Shelley.

TOP RIGHT: No doubt another tall story from the long-chinned comedian Tommy Trinder in the 1944 musical comedy *Fiddlers Three* directed by Harry Watt for Ealing; Robert Hamer produced.

BOTTOM: 'Underneath the Arches' is a number that will always be associated with this duo from the Crazy Gang — fur-coated Bud Flanagan and Chesney Allen. Adding zest to this 1944 comedy, *Dreaming*, produced and directed by John Baxter, were a number of personalities of the day including Teddy Brown, Reginald Foort, Gordon Richards, Raymond Glendenning and Alfredo Campoli.

ABOVE: Child-star Sally Ann Howes, daughter of comedian Bobby Howes, in *The Halfway House.*

TOP LEFT: Ghostly characters of a father and daughter killed in an air-raid, returned to haunt the screen in the shape of real-life father and daughter Mervyn and Glynis Johns (centre). Seen here with Alfred Drayton and Valerie White in *The Halfway House*, produced for Ealing by Cavalcanti and directed in 1944 by Basil Dearden.

TOP RIGHT: Former stage actor Roland Culver (l.), Clive Brook and Beatrice Lillie appeared in the Sydney Box production of *On Approval*, also directed by Clive Brook in 1944.

CENTRE: A scene from *Champagne Charlie.*

BOTTOM LEFT: Bubbly Tommy Trinder in *Champagne Charlie* (1944), a Victorian comedy involving the friendly rivalry between two music-hall celebrities George Leybourne (Tommy Trinder) and Alfred Vance, played by Stanley Holloway. Also in the cast were Jean Kent, Austin Trevor and Betty Warren. John Croydon produced for Ealing and Cavalcanti directed.

BOTTOM RIGHT: Three top stars of the 40s, Stewart Granger, Margaret Lockwood (centre) and Patricia Roc in *Love Story* (1944), another popular romance from Gainsborough. The film was directed by Leslie Arliss, son of actor George Arliss, and produced by Harold Huth.

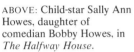

Scenes from *This Happy Breed*, 1944's top money-maker, directed by David Lean and co-produced by Anthony Havelock-Allan and Noel Coward, on whose play it was based. It tells the story of a London family in the peaceful years between the two World Wars.
TOP: An excited family waits for the wedding car. Frank Gibbons (Robert Newton), tries to pacify his mother-in-law (Amy Veness) while his wife (Celia Johnson) calms down sister-in-law (Alison Leggatt). Stanley Holloway, Eileen Erskine and Guy Verney look on. The cast also included John Mills and Kay Walsh.
ABOVE: Director and cinematographer of *This Happy Breed*, David Lean (r.) and Ronald Neame.

TOP LEFT AND RIGHT,
SECOND LEFT: Directed for
Gainsborough by Anthony
Asquith in 1944, *Fanny by
Gaslight* starred Phyllis
Calvert, James Mason,
Stewart Granger and Jean
Kent.

CENTRE RIGHT: Patricia
Medina and Richard Greene
in *Don't Take it to Heart*,
directed by Jeffrey Dell and
produced by Sydney Box in
1944.

THIRD LEFT, BOTTOM LEFT
AND RIGHT: Scenes from
the 1944 production of *The
Way Ahead*, a war story set
in North Africa, produced by
John Sutro and Norman
Walker and directed by
Carol Reed. Seen here:
James Donald, Stanley
Holloway, Leslie Dwyer,
Jimmy Hanley, David Niven
and Leo Genn.

ABOVE: Jean Kent in *Madonna of the Seven Moons.*

LEFT: Phyllis Calvert and Stewart Granger in *Madonna of the Seven Moons* produced for Gainsborough by R. J. Minney and directed in 1944 by top cameraman Arthur Crabtree.

BELOW: At Achnacroish, Torquil (Roger Livesey) takes Joan (Wendy Hiller) to see a ceilidh and from a vantage point in the old barn they watch the dancing of reels and schottisches. A scene from the Powell and Pressburger production of 1945, *I Know Where I'm Going.*

TOP: *English Without Tears*
Michael Wilding seems torn
between the attractions of
Penelope Dudley-Ward (with
jewelled collar) and Peggy
Cummins in these scenes
from a 1944 satirical comedy
produced by Anatole de
Grunwald for Two Cities
and directed by Harold
French. Margaret
Rutherford and Roland
Culver also added their own
particular brand of British
humour to the proceedings.

BOTTOM: Rex Harrison and
Anna Neagle in *I Live in
Grosvenor Square*, produced
and directed by Herbert
Wilcox in 1945.

TOP: Grit in the eye of housewife Celia Johnson extracted by married Doctor Trevor Howard — and there you have the start of *Brief Encounter* (1945). Written by Noel Coward and Ronald Neame from Coward's play *Still Life* and co-produced by Anthony Havelock-Allan and Ronald Neame with David Lean directing, the film became a British classic and an international success.

CENTRE LEFT: 'Do get your 'ands off that fruit Ber-reel'. Joyce Carey affects a refined accent for the benefit of Stanley Holloway and Dennis Harkin (r.) while poor Beryl (Margaret Barton) receives a smart rap over the knuckles in *Brief Encounter*.

CENTRE RIGHT AND BOTTOM LEFT AND RIGHT: Spiv Stewart Granger may be intent on impressing the girl (Joy Shelton), but it's John Mills who wins her in the end. *Waterloo Road* also starred Beatrice Varley, Alastair Sim, Jean Kent and Wylie Watson. A 1945 Gainsborough production directed by Sidney Gilliat.

The Seventh Veil
Muriel and Sydney Box's reputations were firmly established with their Oscar-winning story for this top moneymaker of 1945. Compton Bennett sensitively directed Ann Todd in the role of the schoolgirl who develops into a brilliant pianist under the influence of her guardian James Mason, a handsome but cruel 'Svengali'. It is perhaps open to question whether the psychiatrist, Herbert Lom, was visiting the right patient, but all comes right in the end for both guardian and ward. Outstanding performances from all plus the talents of pianist Eileen Joyce who dubbed for Miss Todd made this film one of the most successful of the 40s.

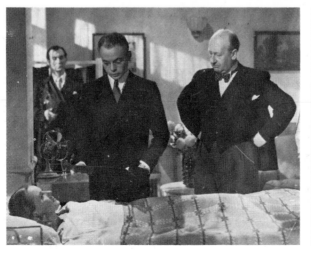

Queues were to form around cinemas and a two or three hour wait was quite commonplace in 1945. Margaret Lockwood and James Mason were the Gainsborough stars the fans flocked to see in this costume piece of a lady turning highwayman in order to retrieve her jewellery. This fast-moving film ensured that the lady would meet a real highwayman and develop into a tale of intrigue, robbery and murder. Directed by Leslie Arliss and produced by R. J. Minney, the film also starred Patricia Roc, Griffiths Jones, Felix Aylmer and Enid Stamp-Taylor.

BOTTOM: Phyllis Calvert, Dulcie Gray, and Anne Crawford were the three leads in *They Were Sisters*, directed by Arthur Crabtree in this Harold Huth 1945 production. The stills indicate that James Mason did not turn out to be the most satisfactory of bridegrooms in his film role, a point which seems entirely lost on actress Pamela Kellino. Not too surprising when one notes from records that there was a name change from Kellino to Mason.

TOP: Three stills from *The Way to the Stars*, a popular film of 1945, set in a small hotel near an airfield. Produced by Anatole de Grunwald and directed by Anthony Asquith, it tells of the servicemen and women who stayed there and how their dangerous missions affected their personal relationships. Jean Simmons sings 'Let him go, let him tarry' to an appreciative wartime audience; John Mills and Trevor Howard survey the damage after a raid; and the inimitable Joyce Carey discusses the problems of the day with Renee Asherson (centre) and Rosamund John (r.).

BOTTOM: Margaret Lockwood and Michael Rennie in *I'll Be Your Sweetheart*, a musical produced by Louis Levy and directed in 1945 by Val Guest.

TOP LEFT: Michael Redgrave in one of the five tales of the supernatural from *Dead of Night*, 1945. This episode was directed by Cavalcanti.

Blithe Spirit (1945)
When the spirit happens to be the ghost of the first wife (Kay Hammond) of well-known writer (Rex Harrison) who then proceeds to wreck the marriage of wife number two (Constance Cummings) then there are no haunts barred in Noel Coward's crisply elegant comedy, directed by David Lean for Anthony Havelock-Allan's Two Cities-Cineguild. With a delicious performance from Margaret Rutherford as the zany spiritualist Madame Arcati, supported by Hugh Wakefield and Joyce Carey as Dr and Mrs Bradman and equalled only by Tom Howard's special effects which gained him his first Oscar, it is understandable that the film was such an immediate success.

TOP RIGHT: Rex Harrison and Constance Cummings hold a dinner party. . . .
BOTTOM: . . . which is followed by a seance. . . .
BELOW: . . . . which produces one *Blithe Spirit* and two unhappy ones.

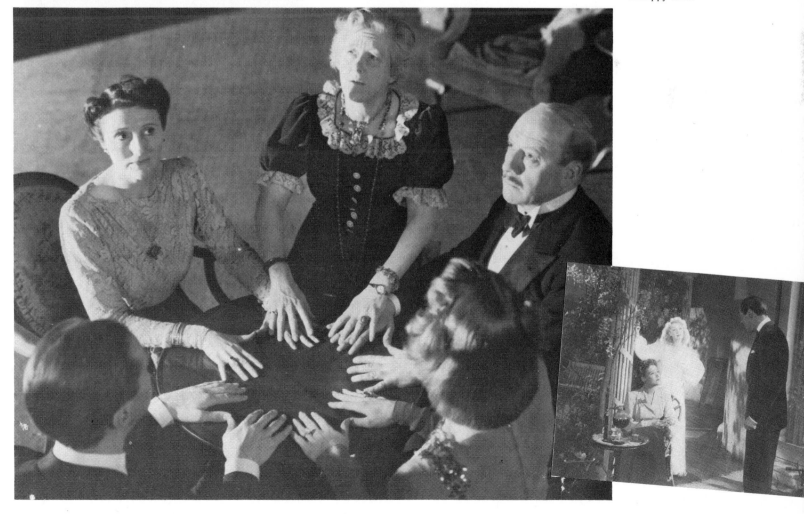

Henry V (1945)
The presentation of Laurence Olivier's highly praised film was largely in the style of the Shakespearian Globe Theatre. Its admirable simplicity, matched by magnificent acting, costumes and splendid score from William Walton certainly made this film a worthy and appropriate offering to the British cinemagoer at the end of the war. These scenes show Laurence Olivier, Renee Asherson, Felix Aylmer and cast.

Caesar and Cleopatra (1946)
Gabriel Pascal's production
for Independent Producers
of Shaw's play took two and
a half years to make at a cost
of more than one and a
quarter million pounds. It
starred Vivien Leigh as
Cleopatra, Claude Rains as
Julius Caesar, Stewart
Granger as Apollodorus and
Flora Robson as Ftatateeta.
Also in the cast were Francis
L. Sullivan, Cecil Parker and
Anthony Eustrel.

TOP LEFT: Gladys Cooper in the Two Cities production of *Beware of Pity*, directed in 1946 by Maurice Elvey.

TOP RIGHT: Rachel Kempson in *The Captive Heart*, a war story set in a German prisoner-of-war camp. Michael Redgrave, Jack Warner, Basil Radford and Jimmy Hanley were also in this 1946 Michael Relph production, directed by Basil Dearden.

BOTTOM LEFT: **Jean Kent** Former 'Windmill' chorus girl, Jean Kent entered the film industry in 1935 and became a leading lady during the 40s when she delighted audiences in films such as *Fanny by Gaslight* and *Trottie True*. Seen here in *Caravan*, directed by Arthur Crabtree for Gainsborough in 1946.

BOTTOM RIGHT: Roses all the way for Ann Ziegler, seen here with Webster Booth (l.) and Peter Graves in *The Laughing Lady*, directed by Paul Stein for British National in 1946. Singers Ziegler and Booth, a very popular team in the 40s, appeared regularly in operettas and variety concerts.

Great Expectations, 1946
'When I grow up . . . in a
year or two or three . . .'
Proud father John Mills
explains the intricacies of
film making to daughter
Juliet who, in turn, was to
become an actress along
with her sister Hayley.
Dickens's novel came alive
with John Mills as Pip,
Valerie Hobson and Jean
Simmons as Estella and
Martita Hunt as Miss
Havisham. Further superb
characterisations came from
Finlay Currie, Alec Guinness
and Bernard Miles. Co-
produced for IP-Cineguild
by Anthony Havelock-Allan
and Ronald Neame, this
masterpiece was given the
master touch by director
David Lean.

TOP: The escalator on set at Denham Studios for the 1946 Powell/Pressburger film *A Matter of Life and Death* was christened 'Operation Ethel' by the firm of engineers who built the 85-ton working model. Ethel's speed varied from 30 to 60 feet per minute and as shown here she was able to carry both cast and crew. This story of a crashed pilot fighting, both mentally and physically, for the right to live, had a star cast that included David Niven, Roger Livesey, Raymond Massey, Kim Hunter, Marius Goring, Kathleen Byron and Robert Coote.

CENTRE AND BOTTOM LEFT: Carol Reed's harrowing and deeply moving masterpiece *Odd Man Out*, made in 1946 for Two Cities, drew a soul-searching performance from James Mason as the wounded IRA man on the run, while Kathleen Ryan's underplaying of his girlfriend made a perfect foil for his performance.

BOTTOM RIGHT: Publicity still of Kay Kendall during the shooting of *London Town* in 1946.

TOP LEFT: Cockney capers by two of the greatest music-hall personalities of their day, Tessie O'Shea and Sid Field in *London Town*. Produced and directed by Wesley Ruggles in 1946.

TOP RIGHT: Anna Neagle and Michael Wilding celebrate in a scene from *Piccadilly Incident* which was produced and directed by Herbert Wilcox for ABPC in 1946. This was one of a number of romantic films in which these two stars appeared, achieving remarkable box-office results.

CENTRE: Like a number of other studios, J. Arthur Rank's Pinewood Studio had been closed by the Government for the duration of the war, its vast sets used for storing emergency food supplies. Although his associated companies had invested enormous amounts of money in British film-making during the war, it was not until the derequisitioning of Pinewood in 1946 that production was able to get under way once again. The first fully completed film to be made after the re-opening was *Green for Danger*, a thriller set in a hospital during wartime, starring (l. to r.) Leo Genn, Megs Jenkins, Trevor Howard, Rosamund John and Sally Gray. Co-produced by Launder and Gilliat for IP-Individual.

BOTTOM: *Frieda*, produced by Michael Relph for Ealing in 1947 and directed by Basil Dearden. With the war at an end, an RAF officer (David Farrar) speculates on the sort of welcome he will receive from his family on his return home with a German bride (Mai Zetterling).

TOP LEFT: Cedric Hardwicke as Ralph Nickleby (l.) and Derek Bond as Nicholas Nickleby.

TOP RIGHT: Happy ending for (l. to r.) Emrys Jones, Sally Ann Howes, Derek Bond, Jill Balcon, Roddy Hughes and Athene Seyler in this Ealing production directed by Cavalcanti in 1947 of *Nicholas Nickleby*.

CENTRE RIGHT: John Maxwell, who had founded the BIP studios at Elstree, had died in 1940. These studios, like Pinewood, had been commandeered by the government during the war so it was now left to the new order at ABPC in 1947 to embark on a massive facelift for the studio before full production could be resumed. So, for their first postwar production, they borrowed the British National studios and made *My Brother Jonathan*, a film that shot Michael Denison to stardom. Surely a source of satisfaction to ABPC's casting director Robert Lennard who had enquired from the film's other star, Dulcie Gray, if she remembered the name of a young man he had used in earlier tests. 'That should not be too difficult,' she told him, 'his name is Michael Denison, he's my husband and you can find him at home!' Former silent star Warwick Ward produced this film for ABPC; Harold French directed in 1947. (L. to r.) Dulcie Gray, Michael Denison and Peter Murray.

CENTRE LEFT: The Two Cities presentation of *Fame is the Spur* was produced and directed by John and Roy Boulting at Denham in 1947. (L. to r.) Marjorie Fielding, Avis Scott, Hugh Burden, Rosamund John and Michael Redgrave.

BOTTOM LEFT: Angry miners storm the gates in *Fame is the Spur*, the story of a socialist's political career at the turn of the century.

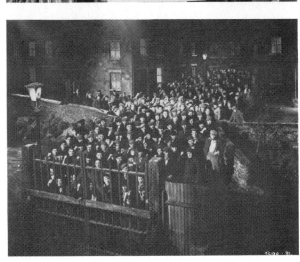

BOTTOM RIGHT: Actor/ director Bernard Miles in *Fame is the Spur*, his 31st film. His previous films included *The Citadel. In Which We Serve. Great Expectations*. and *Nicholas Nickleby*.

TOP LEFT: The Associated British Picture Corporation Ltd, Golden Square, London W.1 in 1947. Today, nearly 40 years later, the same building houses the Thorn-EMI cinemas administration, booking department, theatre operations, publicity and public relations department for Thorn-EMI Screen Entertainment, and is also the head production office for Thorn-EMI Films. The company's film origins go back to 1927 when it was founded by John Maxwell and known as BIP which then became ABPC. Chairman and Chief Executive of Thorn-EMI Screen Entertainment Gary Dartnall today heads an organisation which covers studios, production, cinemas, distribution, exhibition, video and cable.

TOP RIGHT: Dulcie Gray (l.) admires the birthday present chosen for her by Christine Norden while Burgess Meredith looks on approvingly in *Mine Own Executioner*, produced and directed by Anthony Kimmins at Isleworth Studios in 1947. A thriller based on Nigel Balchin's novel.

CENTRE RIGHT: (L. to r.) Patricia Roc, Maxwell Reed, Finlay Currie and Duncan Macrae in the 1947 Sydney Box production of *The Brothers*, directed by David Macdonald.

BOTTOM: **What do you mean, so what else is new?** Peter Noble, who went on to become editor in chief of *Screen International*, is the elegant villain with heroine Marianne Stone in *Escape Dangerous* from a story by Oliver Blakeston. It also starred Beresford Egan and was made in 1947 by DS Films at their Marylebone studios and directed by Digby Smith.

TOP LEFT: Publicity portrait of Anna Neagle and Michael Wilding in the successful Herbert Wilcox film *The Courtneys of Curzon Street*, 1947.

TOP RIGHT: Leslie Howard's son Ronald Howard and G.I. Bonar Colleano both love the same girl — and it shows in *While the Sun Shines*, produced by Anatole de Grunwald for ABPC-International in 1947 and directed by Anthony Asquith from a play by Terence Rattigan.

BOTTOM LEFT: Googie Withers in *The Loves of Joanna Godden*. Directed by Charles Frend and produced for Ealing in 1947 by Sidney Cole.

BOTTOM RIGHT: Jean Kent in *The Loves of Joanna Godden*.

TOP: Jack Cardiff was to win an Oscar for his photography of *Black Narcissus* in 1947. Screenplay, production and direction were by Powell and Pressburger for IP-Archers. The story concerns the influence of the mystical East on the repressed desires of a group of nuns in a Himalayan mission. Seen here are Jean Simmons, Kathleen Byron, David Farrar, Deborah Kerr and Sabu, and the famous bell-scene in which one of the distraught pair hurtles to her death.

BOTTOM: Wedding day for the first in a long line of British Hanoverian kings-to-be (Peter Bull). His sad lady (Joan Greenwood) falls in love with a handsome count (Stewart Granger) but is betrayed by a countess (Flora Robson) in *Saraband for Dead Lovers*, produced for Ealing by Michael Relph who also co-directed with Basil Dearden in 1948. Rich costumes, sumptuous sets and fine performances made this a film to remember.

TOP LEFT: Pride and encouragement are registered by parents Joan Hickson and Bernard Miles in *The Guinea Pig*, as they send their son off to take up a free scholarship at a public school. Hard to believe that the boy was in fact 26-year-old Richard Attenborough who only one year earlier had given another totally convincing performance as a vicious thug in *Brighton Rock*. *The Guinea Pig* was produced and directed by the Boulting Brothers in 1948.

TOP RIGHT: 'They wanted a rag and they got a rag.' Housemaster Cecil Trouncer (l.) in an end of term scene with Sheila Sim and Robert Flemyng in *The Guinea Pig*.

MAIN PICTURE: A scene at the railway station in *The Guinea Pig*.

BELOW: Post-war screen idol Michael Wilding, he of the lovely voice and shy school-boy smile, dances with the ever delightful Anna Neagle in *Spring in Park Lane*. This film, produced and directed by Herbert Wilcox, will always be synonymous with these two stars. Needless to say it was also a huge box-office success on its release in 1948.

Quartet

This film beautifully pinpointed the nub of each of the four Somerset Maugham stories, adapted for the screen by R. C. Sheriff for the 1948 Rank production. Cast with care and precision, the directors were Ken Annakin, Arthur Crabtree, Harold French, Ralph Smart.
TOP LEFT: *The Colonel's Lady* (Nora Swinburne) calmly faces her husband (Cecil Parker) when he discovers that she has written a book of passionate poetry. Could it be remotely possible, he ponders, that this grey creature with whom he has lived for decades has written from experience?

TOP RIGHT: *The Alien Corn:* Dirk Bogarde, whose only interest in life is to become a concert pianist, but who sadly lacks the necessary talent, is seen here with Honor Blackman.

CENTRE LEFT: Jack Watling plays a young man who, in spite of all his father's warnings, manages to avoid, and benefit from, the pitfalls of a Riviera Casino. Mai Zetterling is one of the pitfalls in *The Facts of Life.*

CENTRE RIGHT: *The Kite* may have a very good Minder in the shape of George Cole, but when that care turns to obsession it ruins his marriage to Betty (Susan Shaw).

BOTTOM LEFT: Distinguished actress Diana Wynyard as Lady Chiltern and Glynis Johns as Mabel Chiltern in Oscar Wilde's *An Ideal Husband.*

BOTTOM RIGHT: Debonair Michael Wilding (l.) as Viscount Goring and Hugh Williams as Sir Robert Chiltern in Alexander Korda's lavish 1948 production of *An Ideal Husband.* Stills by courtesy of London Film Productions Ltd.

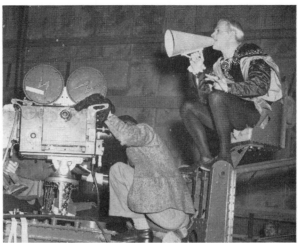

Hamlet

The story goes that an executive, asked by J. Arthur Rank what he thought of the first rushes, replied, 'Wonderful, you wouldn't know it was Shakespeare.' Rank had a passionate faith in the British film industry and invested heavily. Towards the end of the 40s, however, it was necessary to streamline the Rank film empire. Pinewood Films, Two Cities and Gains-borough were now to be called J. Arthur Rank Productions. The Rank presentation of the Two Cities film *Hamlet*, produced and directed by Laurence Olivier in 1948 was the first British film to win an Oscar in the Best Picture category. Olivier's outstanding performance as the melancholic Hamlet together with William Walton's eerie score was fully complemented by a distinguished cast including Eileen Herlie and Basil Sydney as the Queen and King, Felix Aylmer as Polonius, Jean Simmons as Ophelia and Norman Wooland as Horatio.

TOP LEFT: 'I suggest that your whole testimony is a lie.' Sir Robert Norton KC (Robert Donat) puts Ronnie Winslow (Neil North) through a harassing interrogation before deciding whether to accept the brief of *The Winslow Boy*. His sister Margaret Leighton and parents Cedric Hardwicke and Marie Lohr listen with trepidation. An Anatole de Grunwald production of 1948, directed by Anthony Asquith.

CENTRE LEFT: Geraldine Fitzgerald (l.) and Ann Todd in a scene from *So Evil My Love*, a Paramount British production by Hal B. Wallis and directed by Lewis Allen in 1948.

TOP RIGHT: Something of a tail story would be required from mermaid *Miranda* (Glynis Johns) in order to explain the fishy presence of the little merman in her arms. Betty Box produced for Gainsborough in 1948, with Ken Annakin directing.

BOTTOM: Captain R. F. Scott (John Mills) and Lt. Teddy Evans (Kenneth More) in the driving seat, prepare for their expedition to the South Pole in *Scott of the Antarctic*. An Ealing production by Sidney Cole and directed in 1948 by Charles Frend. Chosen as the Royal Film in 1948, its breathtaking photography came from ace cameramen Geoffrey Unsworth, Jack Cardiff and Osmond Borradaile. The film score was written by Vaughan Williams.

BELOW: Dreaded moment of truth for John Mills in *Scott of the Antarctic*.

London Belongs to Me
A number of leading character actors appeared in this Launder and Gilliat production for IP-Individual in 1948, the story of a garage hand who steals a car and is subsequently accused of murder.

TOP LEFT: Hugh Griffiths leads a none too imposing procession over Westminster Bridge.

TOP RIGHT: Fay Compton, Stephen Murray and Wylie Watson.

CENTRE LEFT: (L. to r.) Bruce Saunders, Russell Waters, Andrew Crawford and Kenneth Downey surmount dicey court procedures.

BOTTOM LEFT: Alastair Sim and Joyce Carey.

BOTTOM RIGHT: Susan Shaw and Richard Attenborough.

ABOVE: A delightful portrait of Ivy St Helier.

TOP LEFT: Vivien Leigh and Ralph Richardson in Alexander Korda's production in 1948 of *Anna Karenina* directed by Julien Duvivier. Still by courtesy of London Film Productions Ltd.

CENTRE LEFT: Felipe (Bobby Henrey) watches as housekeeper (Sonia Dresdel) and butler Baines (Ralph Richardson) confront each other at the top of the stairs from which she crashes to her death. *The Fallen Idol* was directed by Carol Reed and co-produced with David O. Selznick at Shepperton in 1948.

TOP RIGHT: **'Please Sir, I want some more.'** John Howard Davies's touching performance in *Oliver Twist* produced by Anthony Havelock-Allan for IP-Cineguild in 1948, was matched but never overshadowed, by Alec Guinness, Robert Newton, Diana Dors, Anthony Newley, and Francis L. Sullivan. David Lean's direction and brilliant adaptation — with Stanley Haynes — from the Dickens novel made this a film for young and old alike.

BOTTOM: David Lean (l.) directs Anthony Newley and Robert Newton (r.) in *Oliver Twist*.

OPPOSITE: Alec Guinness as Fagin in *Oliver Twist*. Former copywriter Alec Guinness studied drama at the Fay Compton School of Dramatic Art, making his stage debut in 1934. He soon became known for his character studies and a long film career followed.

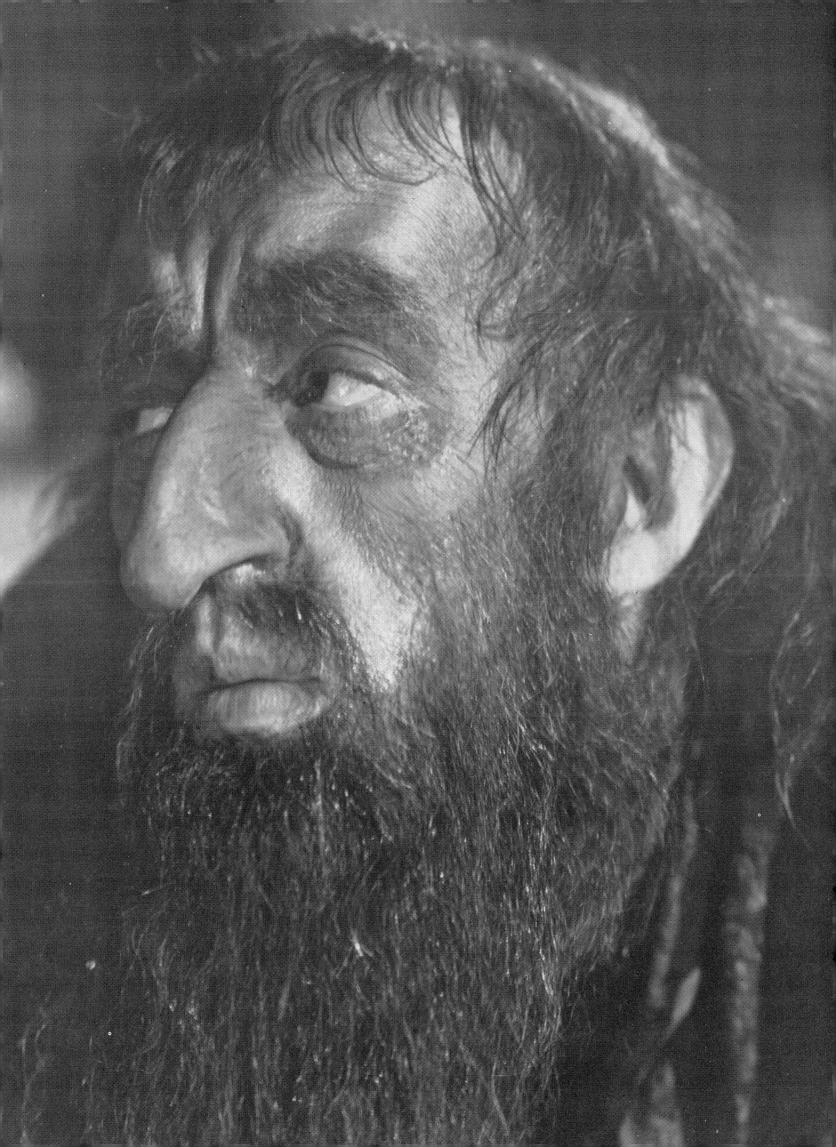

TOP LEFT: We can but hope that bridesmaid, child star Petula Clark, is not doing what she looks as if she is doing at the wedding in *Here Come the Huggetts* (1948). Produced for Gainsborough by Betty Box and directed by Ken Annakin. Other Huggett films followed as well as an equally popular television series. (L. to r.) Jack Warner, Kathleen Harrison, Jimmy Hanley, Jane Hylton, Petula Clark, Susan Shaw, Peter Hammond.

TOP RIGHT: **Associated British Studios, Elstree**
Gracie Fields and her husband Monty Banks visit the rebuilt studios at Elstree on their re-opening in 1948. Modern as they were for their time, today those same studios, now Thorn-EMI, boast a fully equipped nine-stage studio, 27 new cutting rooms, administration blocks, film and sound library service, restaurants, and a new conference/office centre. (L. to r.) Monty Banks, the legendary studio manager Joe Grossman, director Lawrence Huntington, Gracie Fields and general manager Alex Boyd at Elstree.

The Red Shoes
Joy, Evil and Death are all depicted in these scenes from this remarkable 1948 Powell/Pressburger film. Based on the Hans Andersen story, the film gave Moira Shearer a unique opportunity as ballet dancer and actress to express the role of an artist, torn between career and love.

CENTRE: The evil shoemaker (Leonide Massine) tempts a joyous ballerina (Moira Shearer) to acquire *The Red Shoes*, while Robert Helpmann is powerless to prevent the impending tragedy.

BOTTOM LEFT: Once on, *The Red Shoes* possess Moira Shearer. Unable to take them off, she dances on, suffering degradation, despair and, inevitably, death.

BOTTOM RIGHT: A triumphant conclusion for the shoemaker. Having achieved his ends, he returns to retrieve his prize possessions, *The Red Shoes.*

TOP LEFT: *Before* A defiant Richard Todd faces all-comers, unaware of an attack from the rear. From *The Hasty Heart*, produced and directed by Vincent Sherman in 1949 and made by ABPC at Elstree.

TOP RIGHT: *After* Reaction from (l. to r.) John Sherman, Ralph Michael, Howard Marion Crawford, and, seated, Ronald Reagan and Patricia Neal in *The Hasty Heart*, set in a hospital in Burma.

CENTRE RIGHT: (L. to r.) Michael Denison, director Ken Annakin and Patricia Plunkett on set of *Landfall*, produced for ABPC in 1949 by Victor Skutezky.

BOTTOM: '**Did you say one pint or two?**'
Surely the best unsponsored advertisement ever, *Whisky Galore* was based on a true incident in 1941 when a ship carrying a cargo of whisky was wrecked off a Hebridean island, to the glee of the local inhabitants determined to salvage it and the fury of the local customs officials. The fine cast included many British favourites, among them Basil Radford, Joan Greenwood, Gordon Jackson, James Robertson Justice and, seen here, John Gregson. Produced for Ealing by Monja Danischewsky in 1949 and directed by Alexander MacKendrick.

Kind Hearts and Coronets (1949)
An Ealing presentation produced by Michael Relph and directed by Robert Hamer, this classic comedy featured the rare talents of Alec Guinness who played eight members of the D'Ascoyne family (six of whom are seen, top, with Valerie Hobson).

CENTRE LEFT: Beautiful costumes and lovely ladies helped to make this film a winner — Valerie Hobson (l.) and Joan Greenwood.

CENTRE RIGHT: 'Where did you get that hat . . . ?' When not murdering those members of his family who stand between him and a dukedom, Dennis Price finds time to philander a little with Joan Greenwood.

BOTTOM LEFT: 'The wickedest boy in Provence' (Jeremy Spenser) confides in Philippe de Ledocq (Guy Rolfe) whom he takes to be a rich and good man in *The Spider and the Fly*, produced for Pinewood-Mayflower by Maxwell Setton and directed in 1949 by Robert Hamer.

BOTTOM RIGHT: The War Minister (Edward Chapman) rebukes the foppish Colonel de la Roche (Maurice Denham) for offering unwanted advice in *The Spider and the Fly*.

TOP LEFT: Alfred Hitchcock on location outside the Royal Academy of Dramatic Art which was the setting for the Warner Bros-FN production of *Stage Fright* in 1949. It starred Marlene Dietrich, Richard Todd, Michael Wilding and Jane Wyman.

CENTRE LEFT: Unaware that the naked bird on the table is pet duck Clara, Lady Lister (Marjorie Fielding) offers a few words of encouragement to spud-bashing Lord Lister (A. E. Matthews) while butler Beecham (Cecil Parker) decides that discretion is the better part of valour in *The Chiltern Hundreds* (1949).

TOP RIGHT: David Tomlinson and Lana Morris wait for their call on set in *The Chiltern Hundreds*. This sparkling comedy based on a play by William Douglas Home was produced for Two Cities by George H. Brown and directed by John Paddy Carstairs.

BOTTOM: Alexander Pushkin's story, cleverly adapted for the screen by Rodney Ackland and Arthur Boys, plus the lavish sets and costumes designed by Oliver Messel, made *The Queen of Spades* an artistic success of the 40s.

BELOW: Script session for Edith Evans and Anton Walbrook, stars of *The Queen of Spades*, the 1949 ABPC feature directed by Thorold Dickinson and produced by Anatole de Grunwald.

TOP LEFT: *No Place for Jennifer* introduced ten-year-old Janette Scott to cinema audiences, in this story of a backward schoolgirl unable to concentrate on her work as the result of an unstable home environment. Also starring were Leo Genn, seen here, as her father, and Rosamund John and Beatrice Campbell. Produced for ABPC in 1949 by Hamilton G. Inglis and directed by Henry Cass.

TOP RIGHT: In 1949 the National Film Finance Corporation was set up by Act of Parliament as a British Government agency — with an independent Board of Directors — to supplement the finance available to film-makers from British film distributors. One of the first to be assisted financially from the NFFC was *The Third Man* produced in 1949 by David O. Selznick and Alexander Korda, directed by Carol Reed. Since then, the NFFC has funded over 750 feature films. (L. to r.) Orson Welles, Carol Reed and Joseph Cotten on the set of *The Third Man*.

CENTRE RIGHT: Raymond Huntley (l.) and Dennis Price in *The Bad Lord Byron*, produced by Aubrey Baring and directed by David MacDonald in 1949.

CENTRE LEFT: Ealing comedy *Passport to Pimlico* featured (l. to r.) Barbara Murray, John Slater and Paul Dupuis in T. E. B. Clarke's screenplay about a group of Londoners who discover that legally they are part of Burgundy and therefore eligible to have their own laws and taxes, thus freeing them from the austerities of post-war Britain. Directed by Henry Cornelius and produced in 1949 by E. V. H. Emmett, it also starred Stanley Holloway, Margaret Rutherford and Charles Hawtrey.

BOTTOM LEFT: Jane Hylton in *Passport to Pimlico*. She commenced her stage career in 1945 and appeared in 26 British feature films, including *Holiday Camp* and *It Always Rains on Sundays*.

BOTTOM RIGHT: Hermione Baddeley in *Passport to Pimlico*. A former revue comedienne, Hermione Baddeley started her career in 1918, entering the film industry in 1927 in *A Daughter in Revolt. The Guns of Loos* followed and she went on to appear in another 30 films.

The wind of change

1950-1959

AND IT came to pass that television — just a topic of conversation in the late forties — bore programmes and multiplied into thousands upon thousands of little domestic television sets. With the coming of Independent Television in 1955 the number of receivers had increased even more and by the end of the decade had a very marked effect on British film production and exhibition.

The British film industry was also adjusting to the plan put forward by the Government in 1949/50 — later to be implemented — that would adjust the rate of Entertainment Tax in such a way as to benefit the industry. The principal author of this plan was Sir Wilfrid Eady, Second Secretary to the Treasury, thus the exaction became known as the Eady Levy. In effect, tax was abolished on seats up to sevenpence and small cinemas with tiny incomes were exempted from the levy. For more expensive seats, however, the Eady Levy would exact a percentage of tax that would go in part into the new British Film Production Fund, with the remainder going to the Inland Revenue. In October 1950, the production fund received its first cheque from the collections of the levy — started at the beginning of that year — which amounted to £20,000.

In 1951 the film doyens decided to pool their resources and produce an industry 'offering' for the Festival of Britain. Their ideal choice for the occasion was *The Magic Box*, the story of William Friese-Greene, the British inventor of one of the first practical cinematograph cameras. The film, shot in and around the ABPC Studios at Elstree, was produced by Ronald Neame, directed by John Boulting and distributed by the Rank Organisation. The star-studded cast list was headed by Robert Donat in the leading role and continued with a dazzling array of distinguished actors, including Renee Asherson, Richard Attenborough, Glynis Johns, Margaret Johnston, A. E. Matthews, Bernard Miles, Laurence Olivier and Michael Redgrave.

From the early to mid-50s, Ealing Studios continued to make those classic film comedies which became such an important part of British film heritage. Their most famous comedies during this period were *The Man in the White Suit*, *The Lavender Hill Mob* and *The Ladykillers*. Alec Guinness starred in all three of these films — as a frustrated chemist who had discovered a wonder yarn formula, a downtrodden bank clerk who master-

minded a bullion raid on his own company and a seedy, evil-looking leader of a gang of thieves. ABPC were also producing successful, popular films such as the now famous, true war-time story *The Dam Busters*, as well as *The Yellow Balloon, Ice Cold in Alex, Yield to the Night* and *Woman in a Dressing Gown*.

After a difficult period at the end of the 40s, Pinewood studios were back into full production with such films as *The Browning Version, The Importance of Being Earnest* and probably the best-loved Pinewood film of all, *Genevieve*. The story of the traditional veteran car race from London to Brighton was told to the accompaniment of whimsical theme music from Larry Adler's harmonica and starred John Gregson, Dinah Sheridan, Kenneth More and Kay Kendall. The film also had the backing of the National Film Finance Corporation which had been set up in 1949 as a Government agency with an independent Board of Directors to supplement the finance available to film-makers from British film distributors.

Other notable films of the 50s were *Richard III, The Cruel Sea, A Town Like Alice, Odette, The Titfield Thunderbolt, The Kidnappers, Reach for the Sky, Scrooge, Carve Her Name With Pride, Mandy,* and *The Prince and the Showgirl*.

But no amount of fine films could call a halt to galloping television production. In addition, a complex, low incentive tax system, coupled with poor investment was beginning to maim the industry. Shepherd's Bush, Islington and Highbury Studios had been sold at the start of the decade and the 50s were to claim Denham, Welwyn, Worton Hall Isleworth, Warner's Teddington Studios and those of Ealing. It is interesting to note that Ealing and Shepherd's Bush Studios were bought by the BBC, and that Teddington became the ABC Television Studios and later Thames Television.

As if to face the challenge of this onslaught and the modern day philosophy of the 50s, a 'new-wave' school of film-makers was beginning to emerge. Jeans-clad, relatively unknown actors were cast in plays and films showing realistic, working-class backgrounds with 'real' people. Protests against established ideas became the norm and the films began to shock in both action and language. So the 'kitchen sink' dramas were born, and the film fans who had been raised on glamour, music and escapism stayed away. They were not about to exchange their kitchen sink at home for another at the cinema, however realistic. Nevertheless these films had merit, particularly *Look Back in Anger, Room at the Top, Saturday Night and Sunday Morning* and *The Entertainer*. Brilliant young writers like Kingsley Amis, John Braine, John Osborne, Alan Sillitoe and Arnold Wesker came to the fore with their books, plays and screenplays while outstanding directors such as Lindsay Anderson, Karel Reisz, Tony Richardson and John Schlesinger took their proper place in the world of entertainment. Change was the keyword for the end of the 50s.

Last Holiday (1950) was made at Welwyn Studios just prior to ABPC's decision to close them and concentrate their production at Elstree. Here Alec Guinness learns that he has an incurable disease and decides to take that last holiday. The vacation however turns out to be quite different to the one he had anticipated. Produced by Stephen Mitchell, A. D. Peters and J. B. Priestley (on whose story it is based), the film was directed by Henry Cass.

TOP: Produced and directed by Herbert Wilcox in 1950, *Odette* was, arguably, the most outstanding performance of Anna Neagle's long and distinguished career. The film was based on the true story of a woman agent captured and tortured during World War II.

BOTTOM LEFT: Dennis Price and Patricia Dainton as they appeared in the Associated British Technicolour production of Ivor Novello's stage classic *The Dancing Years*. Produced by Warwick Ward and directed by Harold French in 1950.

BOTTOM RIGHT: *The Mudlark*, based on a true incident, has Andrew Ray as the urchin who manages to gain entrance into Windsor Castle and bring a smile to the lips of the mourning Queen Victoria. Produced by Nunnally Johnson and directed by Jean Negulesco in 1950.

TOP LEFT: **Trio**
'So, unless you can learn to read and write, I'm afraid you'll have to go.' The Vicar (Michael Hordern) acting in collaboration with the Church Wardens (Kynaston Reeves and Henry Edwards), tells the Verger (James Hayter) that his illiteracy makes him unfit for his job even though he has held the post for seventeen years. *The Verger* was directed by Ken Annakin.

TOP RIGHT: The boisterous and ubiquitous *Mr Knowall* (Nigel Patrick) is about to bore and infuriate the Captain (Clive Morton) yet again in the second of the Somerset Maugham stories also directed by Ken Annakin.

SECOND LEFT: Captain and guests discuss the short-comings of *Mr Knowall* to very little effect. (L. to r.) Clive Morton, Wilfrid Hyde-White, Naunton Wayne and Anne Crawford.

CENTRE RIGHT: Jean Simmons and Michael Rennie in a publicity still for the *Sanatorium* story in *Trio*.

ABOVE: *Sanatorium* cast line-up of artists who appear in this episode of *Trio*, taken in the grounds of Pinewood studios. (L. to r.) Michael Rennie, Betty Ann Davies, Roland Culver, Jean Simmons, John Laurie, Joan Marion, Andre Morell, and Finlay Currie. Direction was by Harold French, and the film was produced by Anthony Darnborough for Gainsborough in 1950.

EALING STUDIOS presents

JACK WARNER
JIMMY HANLEY
DIRK BOGARDE
ROBERT FLEMYNG

in

THE BLUE LAMP

BERNARD LEE · PEGGY EVANS

A MICHAEL BALCON PRODUCTION
DIRECTED BY BASIL DEARDEN

The Unending Battle of the City Streets

OPPOSITE

BOTTOM LEFT: Poster for Ealing studios' *The Blue Lamp*, the film about London's police force established Jack Warner in the role of P.C. Dixon and later became the long running television series, *Dixon of Dock Green*. Produced by Michael Relph and directed by Basil Dearden in 1950.

OPPOSITE

BOTTOM RIGHT: **'Have you heard the one about . . .'** Alastair Sim seems intent on shocking revelations in *The Happiest Days of Your Life*, a Launder and Gilliat success of 1950. With Margaret Rutherford (l.) and Joyce Grenfell.

TOP: **'Do you remember those film garden parties?'** This *Sunday Pictorial* event always had the fans turning out in their thousands during the late 40s and early 50s. The studio star system was still in operation and the lure of television was still to make its indent into the film industry. Three of the stars of the day about to sign autographs are (l. to r.) Sandra Dorne, Peter Reynolds and Elizabeth Sellars.

BOTTOM: Headed by Michael Balcon and his brilliant team of producers and directors which included Michael Relph and Basil Dearden, Ealing Studios produced a number of comedies which are, and have been for many years, considered classics of their genre. *The Lavender Hill Mob* (1951), for which T. E. B. Clarke won an Oscar for his screenplay, was one such classic. It starred Alec Guinness, Stanley Holloway and Sid James. Production was by Michael Truman and direction by Charles Crichton.

TOP LEFT: David Hannaford looks far from satisfied with *The Second Mate*, tea-sipping Gordon Harker, in this story of a bargee posing as a crook in order to catch a gang of jewel smugglers. Produced and directed by John Baxter in 1951.

TOP RIGHT: The cast of *Young Wives' Tale*, the 1951 ABPC production by Victor Skutezky, were (l. to r.) Audrey Hepburn, Nigel Patrick, Guy Middleton, Joan Greenwood, Derek Farr and Helen Cherry. Henry Cass directed.

CENTRE LEFT: '**So you want to be in pictures . . .**' The 1950 ABPC Elstree Studios Christmas party line-up (l. to r.) Thora Hird, Janette Scott, Joan Dowling, Richard Todd, Beatrice Campbell, Nigel Patrick, Audrey Hepburn, Guy Middleton, Sandra Dorne, Peter Reynolds, Joan Greenwood, Derek Farr and Helen Cherry. The little girl on the left is child actress Janette Scott who appeared in *No Place for Jennifer* and was then groomed for stardom by ABPC during the 50s. Her many films included *The Magic Box. The Lady is a Square* and *The Devil's Disciple.*

CENTRE RIGHT: Two years later the pigtails have dis-appeared for teenager Janette Scott surrounded by ABPC merrymakers, inclu-ding Bob Monkhouse, Jeremy Spenser, John Fraser, Dennis Goodwin, Maureen Swanson.

BOTTOM LEFT: A girl's best friend is her mother — in this case Thora Hird greeting her real life daughter Janette Scott on her return from filming on location, 1955.

BOTTOM RIGHT: A star is born . . . 18-year-old Janette Scott prepares for the premiere of *The Good Companions* in 1957.

TOP LEFT: Moving pictures! British film pioneer William Friese-Greene (Robert Donat) demonstrates his *Magic Box* to an incredulous London bobby (Laurence Olivier). For the 1951 Festival of Britain, the film doyens decided to pool their resources and produce an industry offering for the occasion. *The Magic Box*, the story of William Friese-Greene, inventor of one of the first practical cinematograph cameras, was their choice, with Robert Donat in the lead and with a star cast that included cameo appearances from most of the top stars of the day. It was made in and around the ABPC studios, produced by Ronald Neame and directed by John Boulting. The screenplay was written by Eric Ambler.

TOP CENTRE: Richard Attenborough, as Friese-Greene's young assistant takes his fiancee May Jones (Glynis Johns) and her friend (Margaret Johnston, centre) to see the laboratory where he works and where they are startled by the pioneer's latest invention.

ABOVE: Renee Asherson in *The Magic Box*

CENTRE LEFT: Her Majesty Queen Elizabeth visiting the Elstree set of *The Magic Box* accompanied by Michael Balcon (l.) and John Boulting.

BOTTOM LEFT: A George Higgins portrait of Sybil Thorndike as she appeared in the guest role of one of Friese-Greene's aristocratic clients in *The Magic Box.*

BOTTOM RIGHT: Sheila Sim in *The Magic Box.*

TOP LEFT: Alexander MacKendrick's 1951 classic *The Man in the White Suit* is the story of a chemist discovering what appears to be an indestructible fibre — much to the horror of the hard-headed yarn manufacturers. (L. to r.) Howard Marion Crawford, Alec Guinness, Michael Gough, Cecil Parker, Ernest Thesiger behind the desk. One of the Ealing comedies produced by Sidney Cole.

TOP RIGHT:
The Browning Version.
Michael Redgrave gave a memorable performance as the retiring schoolmaster whose wife, played by Jean Kent, considers him a bore and a failure. Produced by Teddy Baird in 1951, the film was sensitively directed by Anthony Asquith.

SECOND LEFT: Yusef (Ferdy Mayne), the *Hotel Sahara* major-domo, watches as proprietor Emad (Peter Ustinov) turns on the charm for the Italian Capitano (Guido Lorraine), who, with his detachment has just arrived. Produced by George Brown and directed by Ken Annakin in 1951, the cast also included Yvonne de Carlo, David Tomlinson, Roland Culver, Albert Lieven and Bill Owen.

THIRD LEFT: 'Yes dear . . . No dear! Really dear . . . Oh dear . . . Goodbye dear . . .' Alastair Sim as a retired Army officer and secret author of blood-and-thunder novels chats with his fiancee played by Joyce Grenfell while his secretary (Eleanor Summerfield) looks on jealously. A Mario Zampi, ABPC comedy of 1951, *Laughter in Paradise* was the year's top moneymaker. The cast also included Fay Compton, Beatrice Campbell, Anthony Steel, George Cole, Ernest Thesiger, Veronica Hurst and Audrey Hepburn.

BOTTOM LEFT: *Laughter in Paradise* for newly-weds Beatrice Campbell and Guy Middleton.

BOTTOM RIGHT: Joyce Grenfell as Alastair Sim's fiancee Elizabeth in *Laughter in Paradise.*

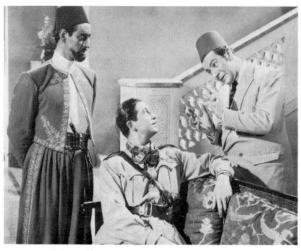

TOP: A case of driving ambition for David Niven and Patricia Dainton, with (l. to r.) Cesar Romero, Vera-Ellen, Richard Todd and Diane Hart, hellbent on raising a lot of money at a charity event in 1951.

BOTTOM LEFT: Studio portrait of Pamela Brown and Hugh Sinclair in *The Second Mrs Tanqueray*, directed in 1952 by Dallas Bower and produced by Roger Proudlock.

CENTRE RIGHT:
'Studying form . . .'
A. E. Matthews, Anthony Steel and Moira Lister try to understand the tax returns for their roving restaurant in *Something Money Can't Buy*, produced by Joseph Janni and directed in 1952 by Pat Jackson for the Rank Organisation.

BOTTOM RIGHT:
Angels One Five
Terence Longden (centre) introduces his parents (Charles Cullum, Ambrosine Philpotts) to their host, Commanding Officer Group Captain Small (Jack Hawkins) in this Associated British presentation, directed by George More O'Ferrall and produced by John Gossage and Derek Twist in 1952. Derek Twist's contribution to the film must have been invaluable; between 1940-45 he served with the RAF during which time he had formed and managed the RAF Film Unit.

TOP LEFT: Richard Attenborough and Diane Hart in *Father's Doing Fine*, a 1952 comedy produced by Victor Skutezky and directed by Henry Cass.

TOP RIGHT: Obviously an amusing experience for Audrey Hepburn, seen here watching radio comedian and scriptwriter Bob Monkhouse typing the script for *Calling All Forces*, in between takes for his film debut in *Secret People*. Produced by Sidney Cole and directed by Thorold Dickinson in 1952.

BOTTOM LEFT:
'A Handbag . . . ?!'
Outraged indignation at the mere mention of such a mundane object as expressed by Lady Bracknell (Edith Evans) in Oscar Wilde's *The Importance of Being Earnest*, beautifully directed by Anthony Asquith and produced by Teddy Baird for BFM-Javelin at Pinewood studios in 1952.

CENTRE RIGHT: Not just any handbag, but one that will establish the true identity of Jack Worthing (Michael Redgrave) as certain initials are pointed out by Miss Prism (Margaret Rutherford) in *The Importance of Being Earnest*.

BOTTOM RIGHT: *The Importance of Being Earnest* having been established, (l. to r.) Michael Redgrave, Joan Greenwood, Dorothy Tutin, and Michael Denison seem content to let nature run its course.

TOP: **Joan Collins**
This 18-year-old starlet had recently signed a long-term contract with the Rank Organisation, when she appeared in *I Believe in You* in 1952 as a youthful offender who is placed on probation.

BELOW: Ada Reeve, stalwart British character actress in *I Believe in You* (1952), produced at Ealing by Michael Relph and directed by Basil Dearden.

BOTTOM: Laurence Harvey (l.) with Harry Fowler in a scene from *I Believe in You*, the story of a probation officer who tries to prevent a young delinquent from returning to a life of crime.

TOP LEFT: **Mandy**
Christine (Phyllis Calvert) hears her daughter Mandy (Mandy Miller) speak for the first time as the headmaster of the school for deaf children (Jack Hawkins) makes the essential first break-through. Produced by Leslie Norman and directed by Alexander MacKendrick for Ealing in 1952, the film made stars of Mandy Miller, a seven-year-old newcomer to films, and Jack Hawkins, who had been appearing in them for nearly twenty years.

TOP RIGHT: Publicity still of Elizabeth Sellars who appeared in *The Gentle Gunman*.

CENTRE LEFT: (L. to r.) John Mills, Dirk Bogarde, Joseph Tomelty and Gilbert Harding in *The Gentle Gunman*, an Ealing presentation, directed by Basil Dearden and produced by Michael Relph in 1952.

BOTTOM: Lobby card for *Castle in the Air*, a comedy about coal board officials and a rich American vying for the purchase of a castle in Scotland. (L. to r.) Helen Cherry, David Tomlinson and Brian Oulton. Produced by Edward Dryhurst and Ernest Gartside and directed by Henry Cass in 1952.

ASSOCIATED BRITISH presents
DAVID TOMLINSON
HELEN CHERRY and
MARGARET RUTHERFORD

CASTLE IN THE AIR ·U·

with BARBARA KELLY
A. E. MATTHEWS
PATRICIA DAINTON
BRIAN OULTON
and EWAN ROBERTS

A HALLMARK PRODUCTION · Screenplay by ALAN MELVILLE · Produced by EDWARD DRYHURST and ERNEST GARTSIDE · Directed by HENRY CASS · Distributed by ASSOCIATED BRITISH-PATHE LTD.

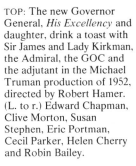

TOP: The new Governor General, *His Excellency* and daughter, drink a toast with Sir James and Lady Kirkman, the Admiral, the GOC and the adjutant in the Michael Truman production of 1952, directed by Robert Hamer. (L. to r.) Edward Chapman, Clive Morton, Susan Stephen, Eric Portman, Cecil Parker, Helen Cherry and Robin Bailey.

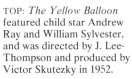

TOP: *The Yellow Balloon* featured child star Andrew Ray and William Sylvester, and was directed by J. Lee-Thompson and produced by Victor Skutezky in 1952.

BELOW: Ernest Thesiger appeared in the 1953 production by Monja Danischewsky of *Meet Mr Lucifer*, directed by Anthony Pelissier for Ealing. Thesiger, elder statesman of the British film industry, started his film career in 1916, and made over 30 films which included *A Little Bit of Fluff*, *Henry V* and *The Man in the White Suit*.

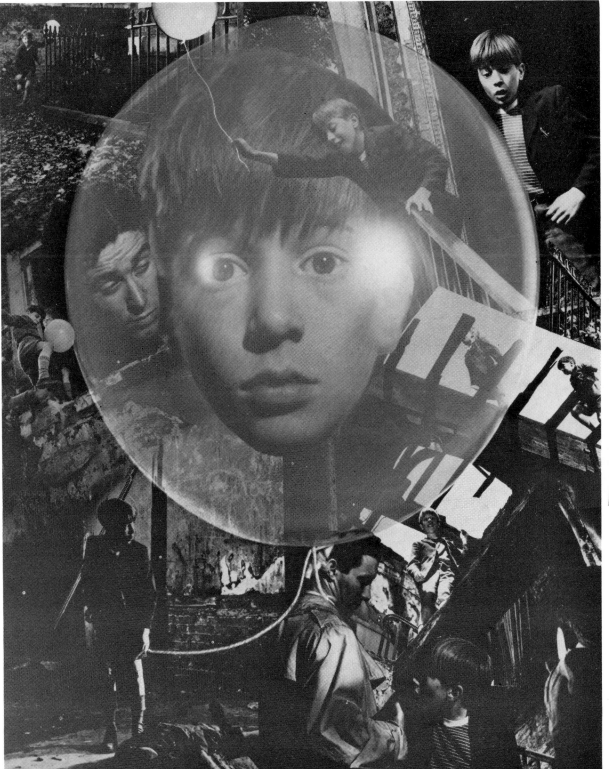

TOP LEFT: Veteran star of stage and screen Donald Wolfit and former stage comedienne Eleanor Summerfield add a touch of grandeur to this ABPC family comedy of *Isn't Life Wonderful!* (1953), produced by Patrick Ward and directed by Harold French.

TOP RIGHT: A touch of competition for Wolfit and Summerfield as Cecil Parker and Eileen Herlie turn out in style for *Isn't Life Wonderful!*

BELOW: Swinging Kay Kendall in *Genevieve*, produced and directed by Henry Cornelius in 1953.

CENTRE RIGHT: One of the many films to receive part of its finance from the NFFC was *Genevieve*, the story of the traditional veteran car race from London to Brighton. Delightful performances from (l. to r.) John Gregson, Dinah Sheridan, Kenneth More and Kay Kendall, plus the whimsical theme music from Larry Adler's harmonica made this comedy a sure winner at the box office.

BOTTOM: Richard Todd as *Rob Roy, The Highland Rogue*, produced by Perce Pearce for Walt Disney and directed by Harold French in 1953.

TOP LEFT: Jack Hawkins, Ava Gardner, and Diana Dors being presented to Her Majesty the Queen at the premiere of *The Cruel Sea*, the top moneymaker of 1953.

CENTRE LEFT: Jack Hawkins in Nicholas Montserrat's *The Cruel Sea* (1952), produced for Ealing by Leslie Norman and directed by Charles Frend. An excellent supporting cast included Donald Sinden, Virginia McKenna and Denholm Elliott.

TOP RIGHT: *The Cruel Sea.*

BOTTOM: Filming *Duel in the Jungle* at the ABPC studios, Elstree.

BELOW: 'If I let him go, will you forgive me?' Perry Henderson (David Farrar) bargains with his fiancee Marion (Jeanne Crain) when she discovers he is plotting the murder of insurance investigator Scott Walters, played by Dana Andrews. A scene from the Associated British-Marcel Hellman production *Duel in the Jungle* directed by George Marshall in 1953.

TOP LEFT: 'Give me a shilling, will you?' asks Marshall, but each crew member goes through his pockets to no avail. A scene from the Ealing comedy *The Maggie*, produced by Michael Truman and directed by Alexander MacKendrick in 1953. (L. to r.) Tommy Kearins, Alex MacKenzie, Abe Barker, Jimmy Copeland and Paul Douglas.

SECOND LEFT: Looks as if the loser takes all in *The Love Lottery* produced in 1953 by Monja Danischewsky and directed for Ealing by Charles Crichton. (L. to r.) David Niven, Peggy Cummins, Gordon Jackson and Charles Victor.

TOP RIGHT: Peggy Cummins in a dream sequence from *The Love Lottery*.

THIRD LEFT: Looking distinctly formidable, *The Kidnappers* arrive to stay with their stern Grandfather.

CENTRE RIGHT: He forbids them to have a pet, so in search of something to love, they borrow a baby that they find in a wood and decide that it will be a very nice substitute . . . even if the baby doesn't look too sure of the situation.

BOTTOM LEFT: Round the table (l. to r.) Vincent Winter, Jon Whiteley, Jean Anderson, Duncan Macrae and Adrienne Corri.

BOTTOM RIGHT: Midnight discussion. *The Kidnappers* was produced by Sergei Nolbandov and Leslie Parkyn and directed in 1953 by Philip Leacock.

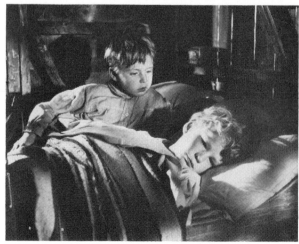

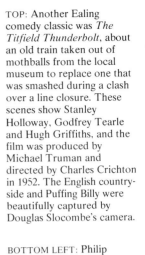

TOP: Another Ealing comedy classic was *The Titfield Thunderbolt*, about an old train taken out of mothballs from the local museum to replace one that was smashed during a clash over a line closure. These scenes show Stanley Holloway, Godfrey Tearle and Hugh Griffiths, and the film was produced by Michael Truman and directed by Charles Crichton in 1952. The English country-side and Puffing Billy were beautifully captured by Douglas Slocombe's camera.

BOTTOM LEFT: Philip Wayne (Jack Hawkins), leader of the first white settlement in New Zealand, bids farewell to his wife Marion (Glynis Johns) before going into the interior. A scene from *The Seekers*, a 1954 George H. Brown production, directed by Ken Annakin.

CENTRE RIGHT: *Hobson's Choice*, produced and directed by David Lean in 1954. 'You'll put aside your weakness for my Maggie if you've a liking for a sound skin.' Henry Hobson (Charles Laughton) prepares to thrash Willie Mossop (John Mills), his boothand, when he discovers that Willie is going to be married to Maggie (Brenda de Banzie), his eldest daughter.

BOTTOM RIGHT:
Happy Ever After
There is the faintest hint of a deodorant advertisement about this still as Yvonne de Carlo turns her attentions to David Niven, leaving Robert Urquhart to ponder that something might be in the air. This 1954 comedy, which also starred Barry Fitzgerald, was produced and directed by Mario Zampi at Elstree.

TOP LEFT: 'Good Pilgrim you do wrong your hand too much, which mannerly devotion shows in this.' Romeo (Laurence Harvey) steps forward in the middle of the dance and takes Juliet's (Susan Shentall) hand. It is the ill-fated young lovers' first meeting in William Shakespeare's *Romeo and Juliet*, produced in 1954 by Joseph Janni and Sandro Ghenzi and directed by Renato Castellani for the Rank Organisation at Pinewood.

TOP RIGHT: Anthony Steel and Sheila Sim in *West of Zanzibar*, produced by Leslie Norman and directed by Harry Watt in 1954.

CENTRE LEFT: (L. to r.) Producer Michael Relph, screenwriter T. E. B. Clarke, jockey Gordon Richards, director Basil Dearden and Michael Balcon on the set of *The Rainbow Jacket*.

CENTRE RIGHT: Bernard Lee (l.) and Bill Owen in a scene from *The Rainbow Jacket*, a racing thriller made in 1954.

BOTTOM: 'Send a few bottles up to my room, Miss Wilson (Beryl Reid), they will do for the old girls' reunion.' Headmistress Fitton (Alastair Sim) shows the new gamesmistress Miss Crawley round, unaware that she is really Policewoman Ruby Gates (Joyce Grenfell) sent to investigate numerous complaints about the school. Monocled Miss Wilson and some of *The Belles of St Trinian's*, participate in the school lab's tasting session. This delightful British Lion comedy was produced and directed by the successful team of Frank Launder and Sidney Gilliat in 1954.

TOP LEFT: *The Green Scarf*, produced by Bertie Ostrer and Albert Fennell. Jane Griffiths and Michael Redgrave in a scene from this 1954 drama directed by George More O'Ferrall. It also starred Ann Todd and Leo Genn.

TOP RIGHT: Kay Walsh chats to director Charles Frend between shots of the 1954 Jack Rix production for Ealing of *Lease of Life* in which she starred opposite Robert Donat.

CENTRE LEFT: Errol Flynn was nearing the end of his fabulous career when he made two films for Herbert Wilcox in the 50s, *King's Rhapsody* and *Lilacs in the Spring* from which this scene is taken. Here, Flynn and Anna Neagle — who also starred in both films — take a trip down memory lane. Made in 1954.

SECOND RIGHT: *For Better, For Worse . . .* Newly-weds Susan Stephen and Dirk Bogarde give a dinner party for the bride's parents, Cecil Parker and Eileen Herlie, while old family friend Athene Seyler looks on approvingly in this 1954 domestic comedy directed by J. Lee-Thompson and produced by Kenneth Harper.

THIRD RIGHT: Natasha Parry and Gerard Philipe in Britain's first X-rated feature film, *Knave of Hearts*. Also appearing were Joan Greenwood, Margaret Johnston, Valerie Hobson and Diana Decker. Produced by Paul Graetz and directed in 1954 by Rene Clement.

BOTTOM: *Carrington V.C.* (David Niven, centre) takes the salute with Major Mitchell (Raymond Francis) after being court-martialled. Fortunately, Captain Alison Graham (Noelle Middleton) is in possession of certain information that will probably clear his name. Directed by Anthony Asquith and produced by Teddy Baird in 1954.

TOP LEFT: Studio portrait of Michael Medwin in *Above Us the Waves* (1955), a wartime naval adventure based on the sinking of the German battleship *Tirpitz*. Produced by Sydney Box and William MacQuitty and directed by Ralph Thomas.

TOP RIGHT: A study in Black and White of high-spirited Moira Fraser in Joseph Somio's production for British Lion in 1955, *The Man who Loved Redheads*, directed by Harold French.

CENTRE RIGHT: Anna Neagle and Errol Flynn in Ivor Novello's *King's Rhapsody*, produced and directed by Herbert Wilcox in 1955.

BOTTOM: A happy band in *The Ladykillers*, an Ealing comic masterpiece of 1955, produced by Seth Holt and directed by Alexander MacKendrick. (Back, l. to r.) Herbert Lom, Peter Sellers, Cecil Parker; (Front, l. to r.) Alec Guinness, Katie Johnson, Danny Green.

TOP: **The Dam Busters**
A stirring march from Eric Coates and a well-paced story based on the development of the bouncing bomb used to destroy the Ruhr dams made this film a blockbuster for ABPC in 1955. Here, scientist Barnes Wallis (Michael Redgrave) explains operations to the air crew, including Wing Commander Guy Gibson (Richard Todd) and to Air Vice-Marshall Ralph Cochrane (Ernest Clark). This Robert Clark/ W. A. Whittaker production was directed by Michael Anderson.

CENTRE LEFT: Well wrapped-up against the weather Sheila Sim visits her husband Richard Attenborough and his co-star George Baker (r.) on location on the Dorset coast, for the shooting of *The Ship that Died of Shame*.

CENTRE RIGHT: Filming in Weymouth harbour of *The Ship that Died of Shame*, a wartime smuggling adventure, produced by Michael Relph and directed by Basil Dearden in 1955 for Ealing.

BOTTOM LEFT:
Oh Rosalinda!!
Eisenstein (Michael Redgrave) flirts with the beautiful stranger at the masked ball without knowing that she is Rosalinda (Ludmilla Tcherina) in disguise. A scene from the Powell/ Pressburger production of 1955 which also starred Anthony Quayle, Dennis Price, Mel Ferrer, Anneliese Rothenberger and Anton Walbrook. The story is based on Johann Strauss's opera *Die Fledermaus*.

BOTTOM RIGHT:
The Colditz Story (1955)
Uncertain of what may happen to them in their new prison camp Colditz Castle, the first British arrivals inspect their quarters. (L. to r.) Lionel Jeffries, John Mills, Bryan Forbes and Christopher Rhodes. Produced by Ivan Foxwell and directed by Guy Hamilton.

Richard III
Olivier's spine-chilling stage interpretation came over just as brilliantly in his 1955 film version which he produced, and co-directed with Anthony Bushell at Shepperton.
TOP: Buckingham (Ralph Richardson) seals his own fate through his reluctance to approve the king's (Laurence Olivier) plans to murder the princes in the Tower.

ABOVE: 'Look how this ring encompasseth thy finger, even so thy breast encloseth my poor heart.' Lady Anne (Claire Bloom) yields to Richard's sinister attraction.

CENTRE LEFT: On location for Seth Holt's *Touch and Go* for Ealing. (L. to r.) Margaret Johnston, Jack Hawkins and June Thorburn get set for the cameras for this 1955 domestic comedy, directed by Michael Truman.

CENTRE RIGHT: (L. to r.) Ronald Shiner, Diane Hart, Ted Ray and interviewer/announcer Peter Haigh, in the ABPC Elstree studio pub, 1956.

BOTTOM LEFT:
Sing along with John!
John Mills and Eleanor Summerfield in *It's Great to be Young*, a 1956 Victor Skutezky production directed by Cyril Frankel.

BOTTOM RIGHT: When young Freddie (Cameron Moore) is bitten by a snake, Miss Horsfall (Jean Anderson) attempts to suck out the poison while Jean Paget (Virginia McKenna) and a Japanese soldier (Tagaki) look on. Peter Finch also starred in *A Town Like Alice* (1956), the story of a forced march by women to their prison camp, directed by Jack Lee and produced by Joseph Janni.

TOP LEFT:
A captive audience
Former vaudeville comedian Benny Hill, was already well-known to television fans by the time he made his 1956 film debut in *Who Done It?* with Irene Handl. Produced and directed for Ealing by the Relph and Dearden team.

TOP RIGHT:
Every story tells a picture
Benny Hill and unseen viewer.

CENTRE: Pitching a tent in a gale makes life difficult for J and Harris (David Tomlinson and Jimmy Edwards) in a scene from Jack Clayton's production for Remus of *Three Men in a Boat*, which also starred Laurence Harvey, Shirley Eaton and Jill Ireland. Directed by Ken Annakin.

BOTTOM LEFT: (L. to r.) Stewart Granger, Francis Matthews, Ava Gardner, and Bill Travers in a scene from *Bhowani Junction*, produced by Pandro S. Berman and directed in 1956 by George Cukor.

BOTTOM RIGHT: 'I'm scared . . .' Susan (Belinda Lee) voices the feelings of all five girls as they leave the nurses' home for their first day on ward duty in *The Feminine Touch*, a Jack Rix production for Ealing in 1956, directed by Pat Jackson. (L. to r.) Barbara Archer, Belinda Lee, Delphi Lawrence, Adrienne Corri, Henryetta Edwards.

MAIN PICTURE: *Yield to the Night* revealed that there was more to Diana Dors than the 'Blonde Bombshell' image she had acquired in previous years. She emerged, in this film, as an actress of depth and perception in the role of a woman in the condemned cell, recalling the events that led to her death sentence.

INSET: Director J. Lee-Thompson, authoress Joan Henry (centre) and actress Marianne Stone have a script conference on the set of *Yield to the Night*, produced by Kenneth Harper at Elstree in 1956.

TOP: A battle of wills between camp commandant Colonel Saito (Sessue Hayakawa) and prisoner of war Colonel Nicholson (Alec Guinness) in this Oscar-winning compelling film *The Bridge on the River Kwai.* directed by David Lean and produced by Sam Spiegel in 1957.

BOTTOM LEFT: *No Time for Tears.* Just a squirt in the eye for poor Anna Neagle as Matron of a children's hospital in this ABPC presentation produced by W. A. Whittaker and directed in 1957 by Cyril Frankel.

BOTTOM RIGHT: *Let's Be Happy* seems an apt enough title for this Marcel Hellman production directed by Henry Levin in 1957. Robert Flemyng (l.) and Gordon Jackson appeared in this romantic comedy with Vera-Ellen and Tony Martin.

TOP LEFT: Eric Portman tries to keep the show on the road, with an audience that includes Mona Washbourne, Celia Johnson, John Salew, John Fraser, Janette Scott, Hugh Griffiths and Paddy Stone in the 1957 ABPC remake of *The Good Companions*, directed by J. Lee-Thompson and produced by Hamilton G. Inglis.

TOP RIGHT: Yvonne Mitchell giving an outstanding performance as *Woman in a Dressing Gown*, a searching commentary on the eternal triangle of husband, wife and the younger woman who threatens the marriage. Anthony Quayle and Sylvia Syms also starred. J. Lee-Thompson directed in 1957 and also co-produced with Frank Godwin.

CENTRE LEFT: It's not the three old ladies locked anywhere in fact, but *Alive and Kicking* in the shape of (l. to r.) Sybil Thorndike, Estelle Winwood and Kathleen Harrison in the 1958 Victor Skutezky production directed by Cyril Frankel at Elstree. Their ages totalled 211 years and they were required to sing, dance, fish, drive a speedboat and be in the make-up chair each morning at 7.30; all of which they did with superb professionalism. The gentleman who did get locked in was Colin Gordon.

BOTTOM LEFT: Looking a little the worse for wear, Stanley Holloway in *Alive and Kicking*.

CENTRE RIGHT AND BOTTOM RIGHT: Director Leslie Norman drew special performances from his cast of *The Shiralee*, the story of a swagman burdened by an unwanted child. Produced in 1957 by Jack Rix, the cast included Peter Finch, Sidney James, Tessie O'Shea and Dana Wilson in the child role.

TOP LEFT: Leaving for occupied France on her first mission, Violette Szabo (Virginia McKenna) leaves behind a photograph of her daughter Tania at the instigation of fellow-agent Tony Fraser (Paul Scofield). A scene from *Carve Her Name With Pride* made at Pinewood studios by the Rank organisation, produced by Daniel M. Angel and directed in 1958 by Lewis Gilbert.

TOP RIGHT: The MGM/ Galaxy presentation of *Tom Thumb*, produced and directed by George Pal was to be evergreen Jessie Matthews' last film. Special effects genius Tom Howard was to win an Oscar for a technique that he had perfected — 'automotion'. This enabled him to split the screen anywhere at all with a line of any given shape. The cast, including Russ Tamblyn, Peter Sellers and Terry-Thomas were to delight children from two to 92 in this Grimm fairy tale produced in 1958. Here, Jessie Matthews and Bernard Miles discuss the problems of wishing for the wrong things at the wrong time in the wrong place. Still by courtesy of MGM.

CENTRE: **Boris Karloff** London born, Boris Karloff emigrated to Canada as a young man and made his way to Hollywood. Although his film career started in 1916, it was not until 1931 that the real turning point came when he landed the role of the monster in *Frankenstein*. From then on he appeared mainly as monsters and madmen filling a permanent niche in the horror film casting spot. His numerous films included *Bride of Frankenstein, The Walking Dead, The Body Snatchers, Corridors of Blood* and *Grip of the Strangler;* the last two films were made in the UK. Here Anthony Dawson (l.) and Boris Karloff survey a head-less chest in *Grip of the Strangler* produced by John Croydon and directed by Robert Day in 1958.

BOTTOM: Ian Bannen congratulates the newly engaged couple Tony Britton and Vanessa Redgrave while Father (Michael Redgrave) looks on in a scene from *Behind the Mask*, a tense drama of hospital life, produced by Sergei Nolbandov and directed by Brian Desmond Hurst in 1958.

TOP: (L. to r.)
Sylvia Syms, Harry Andrews, Anthony Quayle and John Mills appeared in an effective war drama *Ice Cold in Alex*, the story of a military team who drive across the desert after the fall of Tobruk. J. Lee-Thompson's direction ensured that the film's deepening relationships and tensions were kept just at the right pressure. W. A. Whittaker produced for ABPC in 1958.

CENTRE RIGHT: It's not all glamour being a film star. John Mills sips a much needed 'cuppa', supported by a visit from his wife, Mary and fellow thespian Bryan Forbes on the set of *Ice Cold in Alex*.

BOTTOM LEFT: George Baker and Sylvia Syms in the swashbuckling *Moonraker*, a Hamilton G. Inglis production for ABPC in 1958 directed by David MacDonald.

BOTTOM RIGHT: On location for *Moonraker*.

TOP LEFT: Sydney Carton (Dirk Bogarde) bids goodbye to Lucie (Dorothy Tutin) the woman he loves. Her husband has been sentenced by the French Revolutionary Tribunal to the guillotine and Carton plans to save him by exchanging places in prison and dying for him. A scene from *A Tale of Two Cities*, produced for the Rank Organisation by Betty Box and directed in 1958 by Ralph Thomas.

TOP RIGHT: Athene Seyler plays Miss Pross, the vigilant companion of Lucie Manette (Dorothy Tutin) in Dickens' immortal classic *A Tale of Two Cities*.

BOTTOM: The people of Paris jeer as fresh victims for the guillotine are driven to their deaths. This scene was shot on location in Bourges, Central France.

BELOW: Dress designer Beatrice Dawson (centre) advises producer Betty Box and director Ralph Thomas on the gown that Dorothy Tutin will wear for the next day's shooting in *A Tale of Two Cities*.

TOP LEFT: Tory agent with Tory candidate and Tory girl-friend. (L. to r.) Richard Wattis, Ian Carmichael, Moyra Fraser in *Left, Right and Centre*, a Launder/Gilliat comedy of 1959.

TOP RIGHT: Rival Labour candidate (Patricia Bredin) with Labour agent (Eric Barker) in *Left, Right and Centre*.

CENTRE LEFT: Janette Scott, Anthony Newley and Frankie Vaughan face the music for *The Lady is a Square*, also starring Anna Neagle. Directed by Herbert Wilcox who co-produced with Anna Neagle in 1959.

CENTRE RIGHT: A scene from the 1959 Val Guest musical *Expresso Bongo*, a humorous exposé of show business, based on a Wolf Mankowitz play and starring (l. to r.) Susan Hampshire, Yolande Donlan, Cliff Richard, and Laurence Harvey.

BOTTOM:
I'm All Right Jack (1959)
Produced and directed by the Boulting Brothers, this classic comedy was a great success, in Britain as well as the US. Here, a deputation of shop stewards led by Kite (Peter Sellers) asks Bootle (Michael Bates) for an appointment with the Personnel Manager, played by Terry-Thomas, after deciding to call a works stoppage because of Stanley Windrush (Ian Carmichael). (L. to r.) John and Tony Comer, Peter Sellers, Cardew Robinson, Sam Kydd and Michael Bates.

TOP LEFT: Towards the end of the 50s, a new school of film-maker was emerging. *Room at the Top*, a reflection of postwar life and love adapted from John Braine's best selling novel, was an important landmark of this genre. It was beautifully directed by Jack Clayton, and produced by John and James Woolf in 1959. In this scene, Joe Lampton (Laurence Harvey) drives away with his new bride Susan (Heather Sears) while her well-to-do parents (Ambrosine Philpotts and Donald Wolfit) cast an anxious glance in their direction.

TOP RIGHT: Comedy actress Dora Bryan in *Every Night Something Awful*. But J. Arthur Rank took one look at the title and decided that he was not going to have that outside his cinemas! So the film produced by Michael Relph and directed by Basil Dearden in 1959 was retitled *Desert Mice*.

CENTRE LEFT: 'The Chuckles' ENSA troupe pose around the piano on the set during a break in filming for *Desert Mice*. (L. to r.) Irene Handl, Patricia Bredin, Dick Bentley, Dora Bryan, Sid James, Joan Benham, Reginald Beckwith, and Liz Fraser.

BOTTOM LEFT: A very fine feathered friend, Janet Munro played the romantic lead with *Tommy the Toreador* (Tommy Steele).

CENTRE RIGHT: John Paddy Carstairs (l.) directs a scene from *Tommy the Toreador* which featured rock 'n roll star Tommy Steele (r) and Noel Purcell. This 1959 comedy was produced by George H. Brown.

BOTTOM RIGHT: *The Battle of the Sexes* was a comedy based on James Thurber's short story 'The Catbird Seat'. A Monja Danischewsky production of 1959, it was directed by Charles Crichton. In this scene, Mr Martin (Peter Sellers), chief accountant to the House of MacPherson shows Mrs Barrows (Constance Cummings), an American efficiency expert, around the firm.

ABOVE AND TOP: John Osborne's *Look Back in Anger*, produced by Harry Saltzman and Gordon L. T. Scott under the excellent direction of Tony Richardson in 1959 was another example of the new approach to filming in the 50s, and was to signal many changes between the established type of film entertainment and the realistic modern film drama. Its excellent star cast included Richard Burton, Claire Bloom (top centre), Edith Evans (top right) and Mary Ure.

CENTRE: (L. to r.) Lauren Bacall, Kenneth More and producer Marcel Hellman on location for *North West Frontier*. Kenneth More played the role of Captain Scott, an Indian Army Officer who takes a battered, antiquated train through 300 miles of enemy territory during the Indian rebellion at the turn of the century. Produced for the Rank Organisation by Marcel Hellman it was directed in 1959 by J. Lee-Thompson at Pinewood Studios.

BOTTOM: This wall was specially built on location in India for the filming of *North West Frontier*.

The new~ wave swinging sixties

THE SOCIAL and economic changes that had shaken but not stirred the 50s echoed into the 60s. Reality being the essence of the new-wave style, entertainment was sought and found. As society became more permissive in the 60s, then so did the cinema. As Government sex scandals, horrendous murders and other violence hit the headlines, then scenes dealing with these subjects became more explicit. In the 50s, the X film certificate (admittance restricted to persons over 18 years of age) had already been introduced by the British Board of Film Censors, concerned for the welfare of young people.

Responsible 'new-wave' writers and dramatists, however, continued to flourish, as did the vital 'new-wave' directors. Their talents were clearly visible in films such as *A Taste of Honey, The Loneliness of the Long Distance Runner, A Kind of Loving, Billy Liar* and *The Angry Silence*. Richard Attenborough, Alan Bates, Dora Bryan, Tom Courtenay, Richard Harris, June Ritchie, Rachel Roberts and Rita Tushingham were among the actors who made their mark in these films.

Upheavals in the social and political scene also affected the tastes of the film fan. Although cinema admissions were drastically declining, these films, and their stars, were given an enthusiastic reception, particularly by younger, discriminating age-groups. But the disintegration of mass cinema audiences was already more than noticeable, and now exhibitors began to consider the viability of smaller, but packed cinemas in preference to the half-empty, larger ones; thus 'twinning' came into operation, whereby some of the larger cinemas were converted into two smaller units.

Pop music was to play its own special role during this era. The fans queued around the ABPC Elstree studios to catch a glimpse of heartthrob Cliff Richard, there to make *The Young Ones*, the first of a number of successful musicals. Tommy Steele and other rock 'n' roll heroes also featured in films, attracting large audiences. A legend within their own lifetime, the outstanding success of the Beatles was to have an extraordinary effect on the teenagers and music of the day and, not surprisingly, they flocked to see *A Hard Day's Night*.

Comedy was also well catered for by the appearance of double-jointed star Norman Wisdom in a number of films including *On the Beat*, and chubby ''Ello My Darlins' Charlie Drake in *Sands of the Desert* and *Petticoat Pirates*. Popular radio comedians Jimmy Edwards, Tony Hancock, Terry-Thomas and former variety hall artists Morecambe and Wise all featured in films aimed at extending their radio and television popularity to the big screen.

The inimitable 'Carry On' comedy series with its team of stock players that included Sidney James, Kenneth Williams, Kenneth Connor, Charles Hawtrey, Jim Dale, Joan Sims, Hattie Jacques, Barbara Windsor and many others, became firmly established with such titles as *Carry On Jack* and *Carry On Again Doctor*; its popularity is undiminished twenty years later. Maintaining their appeal just as strongly were the 'Doctor' films with Dirk Bogarde and James Robertson Justice in top form in *Doctor in Distress*.

The 60s also brought international stardom to handsome, virile Sean Connery in the role of Ian Fleming's hero, Commander James Bond — 007, licensed to kill. The 'Bond' films, starting off with *Dr No* in 1962, were tremendously successful from the outset and continued to be so through the decade with *From Russia with Love, Goldfinger, Thunderball* and *You Only Live Twice*. Linked with them and held in particular esteem by the British film industry, their American and Canadian born producers, Albert Broccoli and Harry Saltzman.

The 'House of Horror', Hammer Films, which had so successfully got under way in the 50s with spine-chillers *Dracula* and *The Revenge of Frankenstein* amongst others, transferred their main production from Bray to the ABPC Elstree Studios in 1966 and continued to bloodcurdle them in the aisles with such offerings as *The Devil Rides Out* and *Frankenstein Must Be Destroyed*.

Specialisation apart, well-known stars and character actors continued to entertain the public although the British studio star system was a thing of the past. Wendy Hiller and Trevor Howard in *Sons and Lovers*, Richard Attenborough, Bryan Forbes, Jack Hawkins, Roger Livesey and Nigel Patrick in *The League of Gentlemen*, Leslie Norman's *The Long and the Short and the Tall; Tom Jones, The Servant, Becket, The Ipcress File, Darling, Othello, A Man for all Seasons, Alfie, If, The Lion in Winter, The Trials of Oscar Wilde, Lawrence of Arabia, Oliver, Isadora, The Prime of Miss Jean Brodie, Dr Strangelove* and *Women in Love* and many others provided excellent entertainment. They also secured their share of international acclaim and Academy Awards.

Tom (Richard Attenborough) votes against a proposed unofficial strike at the factory and is both surprised and dismayed when his friend Joe (Michael Craig), who has been urging this course of action, suddenly abstains from voting. *The Angry Silence* that results from this scene — the victim-isation and sending to Coventry of Tom by his workmates — was the basis of this powerful 1960 drama. The film is particularly note-worthy for a number of reasons; the fine per-formance of Richard Attenborough, whose skills as a contemporary actor (without the props of a strong character study or make-up) came to the fore; the coming together of the formidable talents of Richard Attenborough and Bryan Forbes to create Beaver Films and co-produce their first feature about a highly controversial subject and, very important for the British film industry, adopting a new policy of deferred payment for the artists which enabled the film to be made for the astonishingly low sum of £97,000. Guy Green directed the film.

But, despite these highlights, the attraction of television continued to encroach on cinema audi-ences, and the British film industry was very sick and fragmented by the end of 1969. Walton Studios, considered the oldest surviving seat of British film heritage, had all but given up the ghost in 1961 while the fortunes of Shepperton studios came and went.

Akin to playing Ten Little Indians, there were only four major British studios left in 1969, Pinewood, ABPC Elstree, Shepperton and MGM-British, also at Elstree. And then — there were three. Within a year MGM studios had been sold to a cold storage company — perhaps the unkindest cut of all.

TOP LEFT: Up-and-coming screen star Billie Whitelaw poses for a publicity still for *Make Mine Mink*, a sparkling comedy made by the Rank Organisation in 1960 which was produced by Hugh Stewart and directed by Robert Asher.

TOP RIGHT: Moment of consternation when a gang of upper class 'paying guests' who steal mink coats to raise money for charity realise that they are about to be interrupted by their maid (Billie Whitelaw) after a recent haul. (L. to r.) Elspeth Duxbury, Athene Seyler, Terry-Thomas and Hattie Jacques in *Make Mine Mink*.

CENTRE LEFT: Relaxing between takes (l. to r.) popular, portly (in this case Martell-y) comedian Jimmy Edwards, Arthur Howard, (brother of Leslie Howard) and producer/director Mario Zampi on the set of *Bottoms Up*, a 1960 comedy set in a boys' school.

CENTRE RIGHT: Wendy Hiller and Trevor Howard in a scene from *Sons and Lovers*, the 1960 Jerry Wald production of D. H. Lawrence's autobiographical novel, with excellent performances from a cast that also included Dean Stockwell, Mary Ure and Heather Sears. Photography was by Freddie Francis and the director was Jack Cardiff, a notable contribution to the decade.

BOTTOM RIGHT: *The League of Gentlemen:* (l. to r.) Bryan Forbes, Roger Livesey, Richard Attenborough, Nigel Patrick, Kieron Moore, Norman Bird and Terence Alexander listen to the proposal put to them by master-mind Jack Hawkins; namely that as redundant army officers they band together to commit a million pound robbery. Pace and humour from the pen of Bryan Forbes, with direction from Basil Dearden, this 1960 Michael Relph production for Allied Film Makers was great entertainment and successful at the box-office.

TOP LEFT: Cinematographer/ director Ronald Neame, whose early career included working as assistant cameraman on the first British talkie *Blackmail*, was to keep his admirers happy with *Tunes of Glory* which he directed in 1960. The story of a strict colonel assigned to a lax drunkard's regiment made a powerful film whose cast included (l. to r.) Gordon Jackson, John Mills, Alec Guinness, Gerald Harper and Alan Cuthbertson. The producers were Albert Fennell and Colin Lesslie.

TOP RIGHT: Perhaps the delightful Sophia Loren should also be taking the pulse of Peter Sellers in Shaw's *The Millionairess*. Produced by Dimitri de Grunwald and Pierre Rouve in 1960, this Anatole de Grunwald presentation was directed by Anthony Asquith.

CENTRE: Laurence Olivier as Archie Rice, the seedy music hall artist in *The Entertainer*. John Osborne's play adapted well for the screen in this Harry Saltzman production of 1960, directed by Tony Richardson.

BOTTOM: The moving finger . . . of director Leslie Norman does not seem to have a too devastating effect on his stars Laurence Harvey (l.) and Richard Todd in the Hal Mason production *The Long and the Short and the Tall*, made at Elstree Studios in 1960.

TOP: Going to bed on Saturday night and waking up on Sunday morning with someone else's wife (Rachel Roberts) may be the sort of life-style that good-time boy Albert Finney has in mind, but it's one that he is not able to pursue for very long, once her husband and his girlfriend become aware of the situation. *Saturday Night and Sunday Morning* would rank beside *Room At the Top* and *Look Back in Anger* as an important contribution to modern film-making in 1960. It was a co-production of Harry Saltzman and Tony Richardson and directed by Karel Reisz.

CENTRE LEFT: Johnnie Byrne (Peter Finch) shows Pauline (Mary Peach) on to the terrace of the House of Commons in *No Love for Johnnie*, a story of the loves, frustrations and ambitions of Johnnie Byrne MP. The cast also included Stanley Holloway, Donald Pleasence, and Billie Whitelaw. Production was by Betty E. Box and the film was directed by Ralph Thomas in 1960.

CENTRE RIGHT AND BOTTOM: Scenes from *The Trials of Oscar Wilde* (1960), based on events that surround Wilde at the pinnacle of his career and his friendship with Lord Alfred Douglas. This scandal shook the country and brought him to stand trial at the Old Bailey, resulting in his disgrace and imprisonment. Peter Finch gave one of the best performances of his career in the leading role, supported by a fine cast that included Yvonne Mitchell, James Mason, John Fraser, Lionel Jeffries and Nigel Patrick. Produced by Harold Huth and directed by Ken Hughes.

TOP: A little soft soap for baby-faced comedian Charlie Drake in *Sands of the Desert*, produced for ABPC by Gordon L. T. Scott and directed in 1960 by John Paddy Carstairs.

CENTRE LEFT: The children (Hayley Mills, Diane Holgate and Alan Barnes) do not see the menace in the man (Alan Bates)'s stance in *Whistle Down the Wind*. Produced by Richard Attenborough and directed by Bryan Forbes in 1961.

CENTRE RIGHT: (L. to r.) Deborah Kerr, Megs Jenkins, Pamela Franklin, Martin Stephens in *The Innocents*, a 1961 production by Albert Fennell/Jack Clayton which also starred Michael Redgrave. The film, based on Henry James's *Turn of the Screw*, was directed by Jack Clayton.

BOTTOM LEFT: Pecking order in the shape of Charlie Drake with Eleanor Summerfield pulling rank in the 1961 production of *Petticoat Pirates*, another comedy from ABPC, produced by Gordon L. T. Scott and directed by David MacDonald.

BOTTOM RIGHT: *A Taste of Honey* (1961): 'I take after you,' the pregnant Jo (Rita Tushingham) retorts angrily as her mother (Dora Bryan) taunts her with being 'man mad', while the discomfited Geoffrey (Murray Melvin) hovers anxiously. Tony Richardson produced, directed and co-scripted with the play's author, Shelagh Delaney.

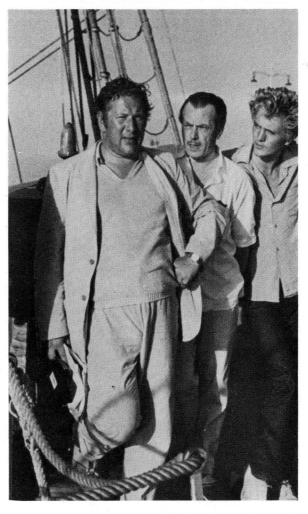

TOP LEFT: Vivien Leigh returned to the screen to play the rich American actress who falls in love with a gigolo (Warren Beatty) in the Louis de Rochemont/ Lothar Wolff adaptation of Tennessee Williams's novel *The Roman Spring of Mrs Stone*, directed in 1962 by Jose Quintero.

TOP RIGHT: Fans queued around Elstree Studios in the swinging 60s to catch a glimpse of their pop idol Cliff Richard, assisted here by The Shadows, in *The Young Ones*, the 1962 top moneymaker. It was produced by Kenneth Harper and directed by Sidney J. Furie.

CENTRE: Hardly a ball of fire, Daniel Massey (2nd r.) with Dave King, Dennis Price and (r.) Norman Rossington seem a little wet behind the ears when it comes to masquerading as firemen in order to elude the police in a bank raid. *Go to Blazes* was produced for ABPC in 1962 by Kenneth Harper and directed by Michael Truman.

THIRD LEFT: The misery and *The Loneliness of the Long Distance Runner* is reflected in the expression of Tom Courtenay in this Tony Richardson/Michael Holden production of 1962. Richardson also directed.

BOTTOM LEFT: A violent quarrel breaks out between Crippen (Donald Pleasence) and his wife (Coral Browne) when she accuses him of keeping a mistress. *Doctor Crippen* was produced by John Clein and directed by Robert Lynn in 1962.

BOTTOM RIGHT: (L. to r.) Peter Ustinov, casting director Robert Lennard and Terence Stamp set sail for a little action while preparing *Billy Budd* (1962) which Ustinov also directed. This 18th century drama aboard a man-of-war, was produced by Millard Kaufman and Ronald Lubin. Melvyn Douglas, John Neville, Paul Rogers and Robert Ryan were also in the cast.

TOP LEFT: June Ritchie and Alan Bates in a scene from *A Kind of Loving* (1962), a modern-day domestic drama directed by John Schlesinger and produced by Joseph Janni.

TOP RIGHT: Leslie Caron finds more than just *The L-Shaped Room* (1962) when, lonely and pregnant, she takes lodgings in a London guest house. Advice is offered from Cicely Courtneidge as well as from other residents played by Tom Bell and Brock Peters. Produced by James Woolf and Richard Attenborough and directed by Bryan Forbes.

CENTRE: The Rank Organisation gave zany comedian Norman Wisdom a double role in their presentation *On the Beat*, produced in 1962 by Hugh Stewart and directed by Robert Asher.

BOTTOM LEFT: With the success of *The Young Ones* still ringing in everyone's ears, Cliff Richard made the musical *Summer Holiday* with its instantly nostalgic theme song. This scene from Kenneth Harper's lively 1962 production, directed by Peter Yates and Herbert Ross, also features Una Stubbs and Melvin Hayes.

BOTTOM RIGHT: Socialite Barbara Murray tells Tony Hancock what he can do with his South Pier Show, while Mayor Ronald Fraser and Hugh Lloyd look on in Gordon L. T. Scott's 1962 production of *The Punch and Judy Man*, directed by Jeremy Summers, son of one of Britain's earlier film directors, Captain Walter Summers.

OPPOSITE: Peter O'Toole as *Lawrence of Arabia* (1962). Superbly photographed by Oscar-winning Freddie Young, this hugely successful epic gained six other Academy awards — for best picture, direction (David Lean), art direction, editing, sound and music. Produced by Sam Spiegel, the cast also included Alec Guinness, Jack Hawkins, Anthony Quayle, Anthony Quinn and Omar Sharif.

TOP LEFT: If you managed to complete *Twice Round the Daffodils*, then you were on the road to recovery — at least that was the premise of this 1962 Peter Rogers production directed by Gerald Thomas. Looking a picture of health (l. to r.) are Donald Houston, Ronald Lewis, Juliet Mills, Donald Sinden, Kenneth Williams, Amanda Reiss, Andrew Ray and Lance Percival.

TOP RIGHT: Our valiant hero Kenneth Williams (in the role of Captain Fearless) appears to have spliced the mainbrace a little too generously while his sturdy crew members Juliet Mills and Donald Houston (r.) look, if not tidy, at least ship-shape. One of the highly popular 'Carry On' series, *Carry On Jack*, produced by Peter Rogers and directed by Gerald Thomas in 1963.

BOTTOM: Carole Lesley, contract artist to ABPC appeared in a number of films that included *Woman in a Dressing Gown, No Trees in the Street*, and *The Pot Carriers*.

TOP LEFT: Lionel Jeffries seems hardly in need of the cup that cheers when joined on set by British born Bob Hope between takes of *Call Me Bwana*, directed by Gordon Douglas for Harry Saltzman and Albert Broccoli in 1963.

TOP RIGHT: Stanley Kubrick produced and directed the macabre black comedy classic *Dr Strangelove or: How I Learned to Stop Worrying and Love the Bomb* in 1963. It starred Peter Sellers seen here with a heavily disguised George C. Scott. Many consider Sellers's playing of three very different roles within the film one of his finest screen achievements.

BOTTOM: The fantasy world of *Billy Liar*, an undertaker's clerk (Tom Courtenay, l.) whose imagination has also cast Mona Washbourne and Wilfred Pickles as chief mourners (centre). The all-seeing eye of director John Schlesinger drew excellent performances from his cast which included Julie Christie and Helen Fraser. Produced in 1963 for Anglo-Amalgamated by Joseph Janni.

TOP LEFT: Simon (Dirk Bogarde) gives the unsuspecting Sir Lancelot (James Robertson Justice) a check-up, but how do you tell the Big Chief that he is only love-sick? *Doctor in Distress*, produced in 1963 by Betty Box and directed by Ralph Thomas, was one of the highly successful series of film comedies based on Richard Gordon's novels.

TOP RIGHT: Millicent Martin and Denholm Elliott in *Nothing but the Best*, a comedy directed by Clive Donner and produced by David Deutsch in 1963.

CENTRE:

A bird in the hand . . .
Tom Jones (Albert Finney) needs no further encouragement from his true love (Susannah York) in Henry Fielding's bawdy romp about a country bumpkin who beds his way to material success. Adapted for the screen by John Osborne, produced and directed by Tony Richardson in 1963, this delightful film of 18th century England was awarded four Oscars for best film, best director, best score and best screenplay.

BOTTOM LEFT: **'Only a bird in a gilded cage . . .'**
(L. to r.) James Booth, Roy Kinnear, Brian Murphy. Stephen Lewis's play *Sparrows Can't Sing* had already been produced on stage by Joan Littlewood when she made her film-making debut as director with this cockney comedy in 1963. The cast also included Barbara Windsor, Avis Bunnage, Barbara Ferris and George Sewell. Production was by Donald Taylor.

BOTTOM RIGHT: Frank (Richard Harris) watches his landlady Mrs Hammond (Rachel Roberts) and ponders the chances of gaining her affections in *This Sporting Life*, a 1963 production by Albert Fennell and Karel Reisz, directed by Lindsay Anderson.

TOP LEFT: *The Servant* is a study of corruption. The story of a sinister man-servant, Barrett (Dirk Bogarde) who panders to the weaknesses of his young master (James Fox) — seen here with his fiancee (Wendy Craig) — until the destruction is complete and it is the servant who becomes the master. Outstanding performances from Dirk Bogarde, James Fox, Sarah Miles and Wendy Craig who were directed by Joseph Losey with an elegantly savage screenplay by Harold Pinter made for a remarkable piece of film entertainment. One of the many films to receive financial assistance from the National Film Finance Corporation, it was produced by Joseph Losey and Norman Priggen in 1963.

TOP RIGHT:
Crooks in Cloisters
Strange habits indeed for cigar-smoking Ronald Fraser and partners in crime Gregoire Aslan and (r.) Melvyn Hayes in Gordon L. T. Scott's comedy of 1963, directed by Jeremy Summers.

BOTTOM: Magnetic husband and wife team of 1963, English-born Elizabeth Taylor and Welsh-born Richard Burton in a scene from Terence Rattigan's story *The VIPs*, directed by Anthony Asquith. Produced by Anatole de Grunwald for MGM-British in 1963.

BELOW: *Wonderful Life* as demonstrated by Susan Hampshire and Cliff Richard in this highly popular musical of 1963, produced at Elstree studios by Kenneth Harper and directed by Sidney J. Furie.

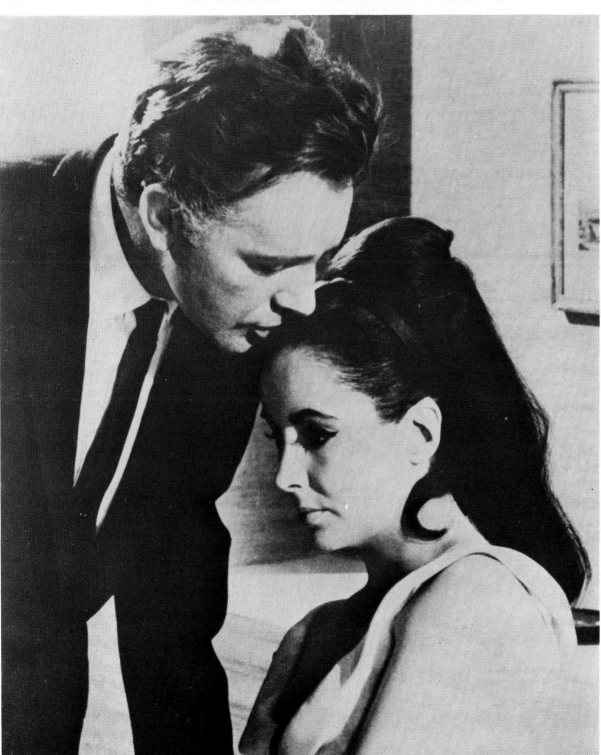

TOP LEFT: Breakfast time 1963 style finds Joe Brown getting a wigging from his father (Harry H. Corbett) on the perils of the 'pop' scene while Mother (Avis Bunnage) provides tea and sympathy in *What a Crazy World*, produced and directed by Michael Carreras.

TOP RIGHT: Rex Harrison and *The Yellow Rolls-Royce:* Anatole de Grunwald's production — one of MGM's top 1965 releases, made at their Elstree studios — had one of the biggest international casts of the year including Ingrid Bergman, George C. Scott, Alain Delon, Shirley MacLaine, Jeanne Moreau and Omar Sharif. Especially written for the screen by Terence Rattigan, it told three exciting and personal stories of the car's different owners in London in the 30s, pre-war Italy and war-time Yugoslavia. Directed by Anthony Asquith.

CENTRE: A top moneymaker of 1964 was *Goldfinger*, with Sean Connery as Ian Fleming's Commander James Bond 007, licensed to kill. For the moment, though, it looks as if the boot is on the other foot as Pussy Galore (Honor Blackman) indicates her intentions. Directed by Guy Hamilton, this Saltzman/Broccoli production was an outstanding success thanks, not least, to the special effects, a lethal bowler and nuclear installations. © 1964 Danjaq S.A.

© 1964 DANJAQ S.A.

BOTTOM LEFT: Beautiful British star of the 20s and 30s, Lilian Harvey became a great favourite of the German cinema. She is seen here at the Cannes Film Festival in the mid-60s talking to Gala's chief executive Kenneth Rive.

BOTTOM RIGHT: The lighting is low-key and the six people sitting around the table are absorbed and intent as Bryan Forbes directs a scene from *Seance on a Wet Afternoon* which he co-produced with Richard Attenborough in 1964. An atmospheric spine chiller which starred Richard Attenborough, Kim Stanley, Nanette Newman and Mark Eden.

TOP: Ken Russell's debut as a feature film director came with *French Dressing*, the story of a reporter and a deckchair attendant who attempt to put their dying sea-side resort on the map by staging a film festival. One is happy to report that Cannes was never like this, but then Gormleigh-on-Sea was never like Cannes. Kenneth Harper produced in 1964.

CENTRE: Peter O'Toole as Henry II and Richard Burton in the name part of *Becket*, a Hal Wallis production for Paramount, directed by Peter Glenville in 1964.

BOTTOM: A scene from *It Happened Here*, which speculated on the actions and atmosphere of a Britain conquered by the Germans in 1940. Starring Pauline Murray, Sebastian Shaw and directed and produced by Kevin Brownlow and Andrew Mollo in 1964.

TOP LEFT: Kim Novak and Laurence Harvey in a scene from *Of Human Bondage* based on Somerset Maugham's novel. The screenplay was written by Bryan Forbes. It was produced by James Woolf in 1964 and directed by Ken Hughes and Henry Hathaway.

TOP RIGHT: As new recruits to MI5, popular comedians Eric Morecambe (l.) and Ernie Wise have a lot of explaining to do to their new boss, William Franklyn while a less than happy Francis Matthews decides that the person who engaged them in the first place needs his head examined. *The Intelligence Men*, directed by Robert Asher, was produced by Hugh Stewart for the Rank Organisation in 1965.

CENTRE RIGHT: The Royal Film Performance of 1965 was the big commercial success *Born Free*, the story of a gamewarden and his wife in Kenya who adopt three lion cubs. Here, Virginia McKenna makes friends with an important member of the cast in readiness for a 'take'. Produced by Carl Foreman, Sam Jaffe and Paul Radin the film, whose title song won an Oscar, was directed by James Hill.

BOTTOM: The Beatles (l. to r. Paul McCartney, John Lennon, Ringo Starr, George Harrison), pop idols of the 60s, had an extraordinary effect on the teenagers and music of the day. Twenty years on, the lyrics and music of these gifted musicians — arranged in many different ways — are still as popular as ever. *A Hard Day's Night* was directed by Richard Lester and produced in 1964 by Walter Shenson.

TOP LEFT: A thoughtful study of John Schlesinger and his star Julie Christie on the set of *Darling* in which Dirk Bogarde and Laurence Harvey co-starred in 1965. Julie Christie won an Oscar for her role of Diana, an ambitious, amoral model who breathes in the sweet smell of success — while working the casting couch circuit — but forgets to exhale. Directed by Schlesinger from an Oscar-winning, feline sharp screenplay by Frederic Raphael, the film was produced by Joseph Janni for Anglo-Amalgamated.

TOP RIGHT: Michael Caine in *The Ipcress File* based on Len Deighton's story of international espionage. Directed by Sidney J. Furie and produced by Harry Saltzman and Charles Kashner in 1965.

CENTRE RIGHT: Poster for *The Knack . . . and how to get it* which tells the story of Tolen (Ray Brooks) who has the knack — and girlfriends to prove it — and Colin (Michael Crawford) who has neither but hopes to remedy the situation at the first possible opportunity. Produced by Oscar Lewenstein, this fast-moving comedy was directed by Richard Lester in 1965.

BOTTOM: Provocative patient Fenella Fielding makes a surprise visit to the men's ward while fellow patient Arthur Haynes seems fairly satisfied with the intrusion. *Doctor in Clover* was the sixth in the series of 'Doctor' films from the best selling novels of Richard Gordon. Produced and directed by Betty Box and Ralph Thomas, it was filmed at Pinewood Studios for Rank in 1965.

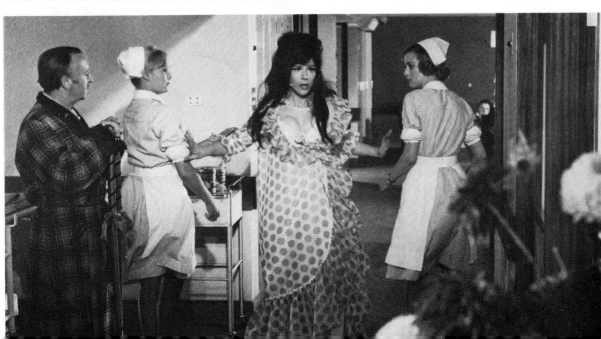

TOP: 'That handkerchief, did an Egyptian to my mother give . . .' Jealous Othello (Laurence Olivier) questions Desdemona (Maggie Smith). The Old Vic is alive and well and very living in this John Brabourne and Anthony Havelock-Allan production of *Othello* in 1965, directed by Stuart Burge.

INSET: *The Nanny* (Bette Davis) tucks the napkin in the collar of Wendy Craig's dress and is rewarded with a look of complete trust which makes it difficult to believe the story of the ten-year-old son of the house that his Nanny is trying to kill him. This Hammer-Seven Arts presentation was produced by Jimmy Sangster and directed by Seth Holt in 1965.

OPPOSITE BOTTOM: Terry-Thomas as the unmitigated cad in *Those Magnificent Men in their Flying Machines*; the story of the 1910 air race from London to Paris. The magnificent cast included Jean-Pierre Cassel, James Fox, Gert Frobe, Benny Hill, Sarah Miles, Robert Morley, Alberto Sordi, Eric Sykes and Stuart Whitman. Produced by Stan Margulies for 20th Century-Fox and directed in 1965 by Ken Annakin.

TOP LEFT: Constable Bernard Bresslaw and David Warner in the leading role of *Morgan: A Suitable Case for Treatment* based on a television play by David Mercer about an artist's hair-brained schemes to prevent his wife's second marriage; Vanessa Redgrave and Robert Stephens also starred. The direction was by Karel Reisz and produced in 1965 by Leon Clore.

TOP RIGHT: This 1965 remake of *She*, based on the Rider Haggard novel, starred (l. to r.) Peter Cushing, Ursula Andress and John Richardson. A Hammer production by Michael Carreras, it was directed by Robert Day.

CENTRE RIGHT: (L. to r.) Michael Hordern, Claire Bloom and Richard Burton in a scene from *The Spy Who Came in from the Cold*, one of the first 'realistic' examples of the seedy, unglamorous world of modern spies as conveyed by John Le Carré's novel. Produced and directed in 1965 by Martin Ritt.

BOTTOM: John Mills directing his daughter Hayley during the filming of *Sky West and Crooked*, a delicate love story of a mentally retarded teenager who falls in love with a gypsy. John Mills also co-produced the film with Jack Hanbury in 1965.

**A Man for All Seasons
(1966)**

TOP: King Henry VIII
(Robert Shaw) comes a-
visiting his Lord Chancellor
Sir Thomas More (Paul
Scofield c.) who, attended by
his wife (Wendy Hiller r.),
his daughter (Susannah York)
and the Duke of Norfolk
(Nigel Davenport), bids him
welcome, unaware that this
meeting is for the purpose of
discussing a private matter
that will eventually lead to
More's execution.

BOTTOM: The King's 'private
matter' is Mistress Anne
Boleyn (Vanessa Redgrave)
already pregnant by him and
insisting on a marriage settlement — to him. There is
however the question of his
20-year-old marriage to his
Catholic queen Catherine of
Aragon to consider, along
with its political and religious
implications.

BELOW: It is left to the wily
and sinister Thomas
Cromwell (Leo McKern) to
manoeuvre England's break
with the Church of Rome,
thus placing the king as head
of the English church which
condones his divorce from
Catherine of Aragon and
consents to his marriage to
Anne Boleyn. Fred
Zinneman's skilful and
authoritative direction
complemented Robert Bolt's
play down to the finest detail
which resulted in six Oscars
for best picture, director,
actor, screenplay, costumes,
and cinematography.
Production was by Fred
Zinneman and Wilton N.
Graf.

TOP LEFT: Bob-a-job week or not, there seems to be a certain lack of rapport between London Bobby (Ian Hendry) and Scoutmaster (Terry-Thomas) in *The Sandwich Man*, a 1966 comedy with a cast including Michael Bentine, Dora Bryan, Bernard Cribbins, Diana Dors, Stanley Holloway, Wilfrid Hyde-White, Ron Moody, Anna Quayle, Norman Wisdom, Donald Wolfit and a host of artists from the variety stage. Produced under the National Film Finance Corporation/Rank scheme by Peter Newbrook and directed by Robert Hartford-Davis.

TOP RIGHT: Peter Cook and Dudley Moore (centre) about to be apprehended by Tony Hancock — as the rest of the mourners (l. to r.) Nanette Newman, John le Mesurier, Norman Bird and John Mills become aware of their dastardly deeds in *The Wrong Box*, based on the novel by Robert Louis Stevenson. Produced in 1966 by Bryan Forbes, Larry Gelbart and Bert Shevelove, it was directed by Bryan Forbes.

CENTRE: The remarkable Edith Evans in *The Whisperers*, the story of a lonely old woman who takes refuge from her drab existence by escaping into her own fantasy world. Bryan Forbes directed this Michael Laughlin and Ronald Shedlo production in 1966.

BOTTOM LEFT: Richard Johnson, leading actor of stage and screen, who appeared in a number of films including *Captain Horatio Hornblower, Operation Crossbow* and *Moll Flanders* before being cast as General Gordon's aide in *Khartoum*, produced in 1966 by Julien Blaustein and directed by Basil Dearden, Eliot Elisofen and Yakima Canutt.

BOTTOM RIGHT: Margot Fonteyn and Rudolf Nureyev in the Royal Ballet's film version of *Romeo and Juliet* (1966), produced and directed by Paul Czinner in five days at Pinewood Studios.

TOP LEFT: A friendly Beefeater shows Michael Caine and Shelley Winters around the Tower of London during their filming of *Alfie*, a role that was to hurtle Caine to stardom as a cockney Lothario. It was produced and directed by Lewis Gilbert in 1966.

TOP RIGHT: Two London-born actors from the cast of *Alfie*: Jane Asher, former child star of such films as *Mandy* and *The Greengage Summer* and Sydney Tafler, who appeared, generally as a 'spiv', in many films, including *The Lavender Hill Mob* and *A Kid for Two Farthings*.

CENTRE: Scenes from the filming of *Accident* which re-united some of *The Servant* team — star Dirk Bogarde, director Joseph Losey and writer Harold Pinter. It also starred Stanley Baker, Jacqueline Sassard and was produced in 1967 by Joseph Losey and Norman Priggen.

BOTTOM: The brilliantly creative team of producer Joseph Janni, director John Schlesinger and actress Julie Christie (seen here with co-star Alan Bates), responsible for the award-winning *Darling*, provided another success in 1967 with the screen version of Thomas Hardy's classic *Far from the Madding Crowd*.

BELOW: Vanessa Redgrave and David Hemmings in *Blow-Up*, the story of a photographer who accidentally photographs a murder. The Pierre Rouve/Carlo Ponti production in 1967 was directed by Michelangelo Antonioni.

TOP LEFT: Richard Burton
starred in the title role in
Doctor Faustus, based on
Christopher Marlowe's play
of 1588. Nearly fifty students
from Oxford University
Dramatic Society were
featured in this Columbia
Pictures release of 1967. It
tells the story of a learned
scientist who sells his soul to
the devil for the love of a
woman. The film was
directed by Professor Nevill
Coghill and Richard Burton
and produced by Richard
Burton and Richard
McWhorter.

TOP RIGHT:
The Long Duel (1967)
Young (Trevor Howard)
meets Jane (Charlotte
Rampling), daughter of his
antagonist Captain Stafford
(Harry Andrews), while
fellow Gymkhana Club
member Crabbe (Jeremy
Lloyd) notes the growing
tension. Ken Annakin pro-
duced and directed this film
based on a story concerning
the capture of a tribal leader
in India. Also starring was
Yul Brynner.

BOTTOM: Olivia Hussey as
Juliet in *Romeo and Juliet.*
This admirable remake in
1968 had all the pace and
style that one expects from
such a worthy group of film
makers as producers
Anthony Havelock-Allan
and John Brabourne and
director Franco Zeffirelli.
The cast included Leonard
Whiting as Romeo, John
McEnery and Michael York.

TOP LEFT: Having been summoned by the Headmaster, the three rebels, (l. to r.) David Wood, Richard Warwick and Malcolm McDowell, await the outcome in *If . . .*, a biting satire on an English public school and the rigidity of our class system. Director Lindsay Anderson drew fine performances from his young cast of largely unknown actors. Anderson co-produced the film with Michael Medwin in 1968.

TOP RIGHT:
The Lion in Winter (1968)
Peter O'Toole as King Henry II and Katharine Hepburn as Eleanor of Aquitaine star in this memorable Joseph E. Levine presentation, produced by Martin Poll and directed by Anthony Harvey. Political conflict and family intrigue about who will succeed to the throne provide the core of this powerful and magnificently acted film. (Top l. to r.) Jane Merrow, Timothy Dalton, Katharine Hepburn; (middle l. to r.) Anthony Hopkins, Peter O'Toole, John Castle; and (front) Nigel Terry.

CENTRE LEFT:
What a bloomer . . .
Kenneth Williams and lovely Angela Douglas in *Carry On . . . Up The Khyber* (1968), another of the immensely popular, low budget comedies produced and directed over nearly 20 years by Peter Rogers and Gerald Thomas. Regular stars of the series were Sid James, Kenneth Connor, Charles Hawtrey, Joan Sims, Hattie Jacques, Bernard Bresslaw, Jim Dale and many more.

BOTTOM: Could it be that their agents are sitting out front? Peter Butterworth and Joan Sims seem intent on finishing their act with a certain amount of panache while Charles Hawtrey (centre) adds his own unsuspecting contribution to this scene from *Carry On . . . Up The Khyber*.

TOP: **The House of Hammer**
William Hammer formed
Hammer Productions in 1936
in association with British
Lion. But it was not until
1947 — when he went into
partnership with his son
Anthony and Enrique and
James Carreras of Exclusive
Films — that the House of
Hammer really got under
way, due particularly to a
series of extraordinarily
successful horror films begun
in 1956. Based at Bray
Studios until 1966, they then
transferred production to the
ABPC studios at Elstree and
for a number of years pro-
duced spine-chillers starring
Christopher Lee and Peter
Cushing. Here, Christopher
Lee plays the 'goodie' for
once in *The Devil Rides Out*
with shocked bystanders
Patrick Mower, Paul
Eddington and Sarah
Lawson.

BOTTOM LEFT: Charles
Gray prepares for action in
The Devil Rides Out, the
Hammer film version of
Dennis Wheatley's thriller
produced by Anthony
Nelson Keys and directed by
Terence Fisher in 1968.
Rosalyn Landor is the
victim.

CENTRE RIGHT:
Isadora (1968)
Isadora Duncan (Vanessa
Redgrave) demonstrates a
dance step for her young
pupils on the lawn outside
her Parisian villa. A scene
from Universal's production
which also starred James Fox,
Ivan Tchenko and Jason
Robards. The film was directed by Karel Reisz for
producers Robert and
Raymond Hakim.

BOTTOM RIGHT: Design for
Stanley Kubrick's *2001: A
Space Odyssey*, made in
deep secrecy at MGM's
studio, Elstree in 1968. By
the end of the 60s — due to
the influence of television
and lack of investment —
cinema admissions had
plummeted to an all-time low.
The closure of the MGM-
British Studios in 1970 was
yet another casualty of the
ailing film industry of that
period.

TOP: **'Please Sir, I want some more . . .'**
Mark Lester made a touching Oliver Twist whether in such dramatic scenes as this or singing one of Lionel Bart's marvellous songs in this screen version *Oliver!* Second-to-none photography from Oswald Morris, excellent sets from John Box and a special cast under the direction of Carol Reed, resulted in first-rate entertainment for all ages and several well-deserved academy awards.

BOTTOM: The exuberant *Who Will Buy?* number from *Oliver!*

ABOVE: The Artful Dodger (Jack Wild) and Fagin (Ron Moody) decide that it has been well worth their while to 'pick a pocket or two' in *Oliver!*, produced by John Woolf for Warwick-Romulus in 1968.

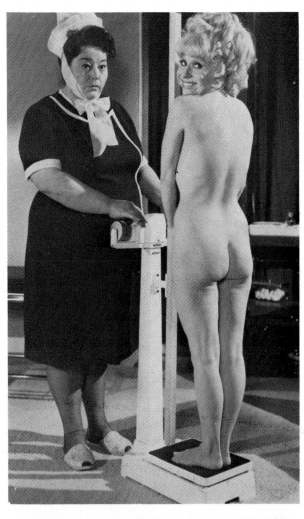

TOP LEFT: Matron (Hattie Jacques) and Barbara Windsor in another 'Carry On' romp, *Carry On Again Doctor* (1969), a not too profound probe into the heart of surgical science, produced and directed at Pinewood by Peter Rogers and Gerald Thomas.

TOP RIGHT: Gladstone Screwer (Sidney James), the disorderly medical mission orderly, introduces newly arrived Doctor Nookey (Jim Dale r.) to one of the local attractions, Scrubba (Shakira Baksh) in a scene from *Carry On Again Doctor*.

CENTRE RIGHT: David Bradley (l.) as the schoolboy who tames a kestrel and Colin Welland as his schoolmaster in *Kes*, a film which takes a realistic look at life in a small northern town. A direct and honest film from director Ken Loach in 1969, produced by Tony Garnett.

BOTTOM LEFT: Scottish stage actress Eileen Herlie appeared in a number of films including *Hamlet, The Story of Gilbert and Sullivan, For Better for Worse* and is seen here in *The Sea Gull*, based on Chekhov's play, produced and directed in 1969 by Sidney Lumet.

BOTTOM RIGHT: British stage and screen actor Harry Andrews, who often portrayed military and authoritative roles, appearing in *The Red Beret, Ice Cold in Alex, The Charge of the Light Brigade* and as Sorin in *The Sea Gull*.

BELOW: Rocket specialist Warren Mitchell (l.) and Bernard Bresslaw prepare for their latest mission in *Moon Zero Two*, a Hammer presentation of 1969 produced by Michael Carreras and directed by Roy Ward Baker.

TOP LEFT: Oscar-winning Maggie Smith with Jane Carr in *The Prime of Miss Jean Brodie*, the 1969 Robert Fryer production for 20th Century-Fox, directed by Ronald Neame. Based on the novel by Muriel Spark, it is a story of a charismatic Scottish schoolmistress whose undisciplined, romantic nature destroys her professional and private relationships.

TOP RIGHT: Richard Attenborough's directorial debut, co-produced with Brian Duffy, was *Oh! What a Lovely War* (1969), the screen version of Joan Littlewood's stage production. The all-star cast included Dirk Bogarde, Phyllis Calvert, Jack Hawkins, John Mills, Laurence Olivier, Michael and Vanessa Redgrave, Maggie Smith, Susannah York and (l. to r.) standing: Paul Daneman, Kenneth More, John Clements. sitting: Ralph Richardson, Ian Holm, John Gielgud.

MAIN PICTURE: Kenneth More (l.) as Kaiser Wilhelm II and John Clements as General Von Moltke in *Oh! What a Lovely War*.

BELOW: (L. to r.) Eleanor Bron, Jenny Linden and Glenda Jackson during the shooting of *Women in Love*, director Ken Russell's screen version of D. H. Lawrence's novel. Glenda Jackson won her first Oscar as the fiery Gudrun in this Larry Kramer production of 1969. Also starring were Alan Bates, Michael Gough and Oliver Reed.

The shaky seventies

BY 1970, EMI had acquired the controlling interest in ABPC Elstree. MGM-British who had just sold their own Elstree studios formed a joint association with EMI after which they were re-christened the EMI-MGM Elstree Studios. The agreement lasted until 1973 when the studios reverted back to EMI. By 1975 every British studio large and small was fighting for survival. Stages at Bray, Elstree, Pinewood, Shepperton, Twickenham, Isleworth, Wembley closed, reopened and closed again. Of course, the industry had seen it all before in the 20s, early 30s and again in the 40s, but that was a long time ago and did not help the current situation. Nevertheless, something of the old pioneering spirit was obviously still in existence as the studios and industry staggered through those difficult days.

Incredible, then, with all the body blows resulting from tax laws, competition from television, low investment and simply from standing on the threshold of an entertainment revolution that would encompass more television, plus cable, video and satellites, that they managed to make films at all, but they did and some very good ones at that. An excellent programme of films had been instigated by Bryan Forbes as Head of Production at Elstree in the early 70s — it included *The Railway Children, The Man who Haunted Himself, The Tales of Beatrix Potter* and Cannes Grand Prix winner, Joseph Losey's *The Go-Between* starring Julie Christie, Alan Bates, Edward Fox and Margaret Leighton.

Pinewood was to continue to fly the flag with such successes as *Diamonds are Forever, Sleuth, The Day of the Jackal, The Man with the Golden Gun, The Slipper and the Rose* and *Bugsy Malone*, Alan Parker's feature film debut. Twickenham Studios also had their share of good films amongst which were *The Wild Geese* and *The Eagle has Landed*.

There is no doubt that investment from American companies into British studio productions created a lifeline that assisted their survival in the 70s. A British film collection would not be complete without mention of the second-to-none British film technology that produced many of the special effects, gadgetry, devices, sets and tanks for the American and British blockbusters, such as the Bond films and *Superman* at Pinewood and the *Star Wars* saga at Elstree.

Up to the late 70s, there had always been a sharp division of interests and politics between British film and television, but as the decade drew to a close, it became clear that the future of the film industry — if there was to be one — would inevitably be linked with the new communications explosion, embracing all major technological entertainment. From now on, the producer of any major film production would automatically have to consider its distribution pattern in terms of cinema exhibition, video, television and cable sales. Feature films were already being made for television and anyone attempting to cry halt was clearly out of touch. Progress was on the march with a vengeance.

Ryan's Daughter
Oscars were won by John Mills for his outstanding performance as the village simpleton and Frederick A. Young for cinematography in this 1970 film produced by Anthony Havelock-Allan and directed by David Lean.

TOP LEFT: An unusual role and a fine dramatic performance from Roger Moore in *The Man Who Haunted Himself*, produced by Michael Relph and directed by Basil Dearden in 1970.

TOP RIGHT: He'll need more than a shilling in the meter for this lot . . . David Prowse (later to play Darth Vader in *Star Wars*) hopes for some high-powered support in the EMI-Hammer presentation of *The Horror of Frankenstein*, produced and directed by Jimmy Sangster in 1970.

OPPOSITE: The Irving Allen/ Andrew Donally 1970 production of *Cromwell*, directed by Ken Hughes was reported to have received the highest sum ever paid by the Russians for a British film at an estimated £100,000. Perhaps this historical drama of Britain's Charles I and his quest for supreme authority, the ensuing civil war and his subsequent execution had a certain appeal. Certainly there was an uncanny likeness between Alec Guinness (l.) and the portraits of Charles I. Richard Harris played the Roundhead leader, Cromwell, who put his faith in God and kept his gunpowder dry.

BELOW: Michael Jayston, seen here as Henry Ireton, the English parliamentarian general in *Cromwell*.

BOTTOM: Dorothy Tutin as Queen Henrietta Maria in *Cromwell*. A leading British stage actress, her many films include *The Importance of Being Earnest* and *A Tale of Two Cities*.

TOP: The persistent decline of cinema audiences continued to have an overall effect on the industry during the shaky 70s. A number of studios had closed since the end of the war and now, with MGM-British Studios closed and the future of several others in question, the remaining major studios such as Elstree and Pinewood and smaller ones like Twickenham began their battle for survival. ABPC Elstree had been bought by EMI in 1969 and Lord Delfont, as Chief Executive, appointed Bryan Forbes as Head of Production. Although the plan was shortlived, a programme of imaginative films was started including *The Man Who Haunted Himself, Tales of Beatrix Potter, The Raging Moon*, and the highly successful Robert Lynn production *The Railway Children*, directed by Lionel Jeffries in 1970. (L. to r.) Gary Warren, Sally Thomsett and Jenny Agutter explore their new home in the country by the railway.

BOTTOM: Colin Blakely as Dr Watson and Robert Stephens as Sherlock Holmes in *The Private Life of Sherlock Holmes*, produced and directed by Billy Wilder in 1970.

The Go-Between (1970)
Edward Fox (centre) plays an aristocrat whose fiancee (Julie Christie, left) is having an affair with a local farmer played by Alan Bates. A young friend (Dominic Guard) is persuaded to become a go-between for the guilty couple. Margaret Leighton (right) as Julie Christie's mother, eventually discovers the nature of her young guest's frequent errands.
ABOVE: Director Joseph Losey rehearses with Dominic Guard and Alan Bates. Produced by John Heyman and Norman Priggen for EMI-MGM, the film took a Grand Prix at Cannes in 1971.

TOP LEFT: John Mills and Carol White in the Basil Rayburn production of *Dulcima* directed in 1970 by Frank Nesbitt. It tells of a farmer's daughter who discovers that the lecherous, miserly farmer with whom she goes to live, is nowhere near as penniless as he would have her believe.

TOP RIGHT: 'Britain's answer to all past dramas of passion in the bush,' said the publicity blurb for *Carry On Up The Jungle*. (L. to r.) Frankie Howerd, Kenneth Connor, Joan Sims, Sidney James and Jacki Piper. Produced and directed, as usual by Peter Rogers and Gerald Thomas in 1970.

CENTRE: A love affair develops between two handicapped patients (Nanette Newman and Malcolm McDowell) in a nursing home, sparking off not only their new found interest in each other, but also a will to communicate once again with the outside world. *The Raging Moon* was directed by Bryan Forbes and produced for EMI by Bruce Cohn Curtis in 1970.

BOTTOM: Not the usual type of bunny girls perhaps, but four dancers from the Royal Ballet in the Richard Goodwin production of 1971 of *Tales of Beatrix Potter*. Five of the famed Victorian author's most well-known stories, choreographed by Frederick Ashton, made for outstanding entertainment. This John Brabourne presentation was directed by Reginald Mills.

TOP LEFT: *Macbeth: 'We will speak further.'* *Lady Macbeth: 'Only look up clear. To alter favour ever is to fear. Leave all the rest to me.'* Jon Finch and Francesca Annis plan Duncan's murder in the filmed version of Shakespeare's *Macbeth*, directed by Roman Polanski and produced by Andrew Braunsberg in 1971.

SECOND LEFT: Janet Suzman and Alan Bates in *A Day in the Death of Joe Egg*, which concerns a family's problems in coping with a handicapped daughter. Produced by David Deutsch, this screen adaptation of the play by Peter Nichols was directed by Peter Medak in 1971.

THIRD LEFT: Not the best commercial for domestic bliss. Nevertheless, Glenda Jackson and Murray Head cope well in *Sunday, Bloody Sunday* under John Schlesinger's direction; production was by Joseph Janni in 1971. The film also starred Peter Finch.

TOP RIGHT: Wistful, wishing and truly capturing the mood of the 20s is Twiggy in the MGM/Russflix 1971 adaptation of Sandy Wilson's musical *The Boy Friend*, produced and directed by Ken Russell.

BOTTOM: Christopher Gable (left) and Twiggy in a number from *The Boy Friend*, which also starred Max Adrian, Antonia Ellis, Moyra Fraser, Glenda Jackson, Bryan Pringle and Barbara Windsor.

TOP LEFT: Two Queens with an inbred fear and distrust of each other, Elizabeth I of England and Mary Queen of Scots. Although Mary will become Elizabeth's prisoner — and eventually be executed by her — it is Mary's son James who will succeed to the thrones of England and Scotland on Elizabeth's death. Here Glenda Jackson, as Elizabeth, takes stock of the situation counselled by Trevor Howard and Daniel Massey (l.).

TOP RIGHT: Vanessa Redgrave, daughter of Michael Redgrave and Rachel Kempson in the title role of *Mary Queen of Scots*. This Universal/Hal B. Wallis production of 1971 was directed by Charles Jarrott.

CENTRE LEFT: Anne Bancroft and Simon Ward in *Young Winston*, producer Carl Foreman's screenplay of Churchill's *My Early Life*. The all-star cast included Jack Hawkins, Ian Holm, Anthony Hopkins, Patrick Magee, Robert Shaw and Edward Woodward. A Columbia presentation directed by Richard Attenborough.

BOTTOM: (L. to r.) John Mills, Richard Attenborough, Carl Foreman, Kenneth Maidment and Simon Ward during the shooting of *Young Winston* in 1972.

TOP LEFT: Malcolm McDowell in *A Clockwork Orange*, the violent story of a thug and murderer experimentally brainwashed and thrown back into society. Directed by Stanley Kubrick and produced by Bernard Williams in 1971.

TOP RIGHT: Alice (Fiona Fullerton) joins Gryphon (Spike Milligan) and Mock Turtle (Michael Hordern) in a lobster quadrille. William Sterling directed *Alice's Adventures in Wonderland* (1972). Derek Horne produced for Josef Shaftel.

CENTRE LEFT: Mrs Wickens (Diana Dors, believe it or not) divulges her plot to murder the children to the drunken Mr Wickens (David Lodge) in a scene from *The Amazing Mr Blunden*. This atmospheric children's ghost story was produced in 1972 by Barry Levinson and directed by Lionel Jeffries who also wrote the screenplay.

CENTRE RIGHT: Laurence Olivier (l.) ridicules Michael Caine in a game of cat and mouse in the psychological thriller taken from Anthony Shaffer's play *Sleuth*. Directed by Joseph L. Mankiewicz in 1972, it was produced by Morton Gottlieb.

BOTTOM: **The Children's Film Foundation**
Award winners and members of the CFF being presented to their Patron, HRH The Duchess of Kent by Sir John Davis and Henry Geddes at the première of *Hide and Seek* and *Kadoyng* in 1972. In 1944 J. Arthur Rank first set up a children's division within the framework of the Rank Organisation. This was superseded by the all-industry Children's Film Foundation in 1952. Sadly, the dramatic decline in UK cinema admissions disastrously affected the Eady Levy Fund on which the Foundation depended for its annual production grants. Faced with extinction in 1981, the CFF board, the film industry, unions and the BBC came together to negotiate an agreement that in essence would release ten CFF films and three feature films per year, which would subsequently be screened on BBC Television. Still by courtesy of the Children's Film and Television Foundation.

TOP: *Surprise, surprise . . .*
Glenda Jackson won an
Oscar for her performance
in *A Touch of Class*, a
romantic satire in which she
co-starred with George
Segal. Produced and
directed for Avco/Brut/
Gordon Films by Melvin
Frank in 1972.

BOTTOM LEFT: Georgina
Hale and Robert Powell in
Mahler, Ken Russell's film
biography of the composer,
produced by Roy Baird in
1974.

BOTTOM RIGHT: Poster for
*Murder on the Orient
Express*, a Nat Cohen pre-
sentation for EMI Film
Distributors, produced by
John Brabourne and Richard
Goodwin and directed by
Sidney Lumet.

TOP LEFT: The cast of *Murder on the Orient Express* being presented to HM the Queen by Nat Cohen at the film's premiere in 1974. (L. to r.) Sir John Gielgud, Michael York and Albert Finney. Photo by PIC Photos.

TOP RIGHT: Albert Finney as Agatha Christie's famous Belgian detective Hercule Poirot in *Murder on the Orient Express.*

BOTTOM: Portrait of distinguished British stage and screen actress Wendy Hiller in her role as the Russian princess in *Murder on the Orient Express.* Costumiers Berman and Nathans made a number of costumes for the film including this ensemble worn by Miss Hiller. Bermans celebrate their centenary in 1984.

TOP: The 1974 remake of *Great Expectations* starred Sarah Miles as Estella and Michael York as Pip. Also starring were Joss Ackland, Margaret Leighton, James Mason, Robert Morley and Heather Sears.

BOTTOM LEFT: Rachel Roberts and Robert Morley in the Lew Grade presentation of *Great Expectations*, produced by Robert Fryer and directed by Joseph Hardy.

BOTTOM RIGHT: Special trappings and *Great Expectations* for Michael York.

BELOW: Publicity portrait of Anthony Quayle as Jaggers in *Great Expectations*. A stage actor and director he made his film debut in 1948 in *Hamlet*. He went on to make many films including *Woman in a Dressing Gown*, *Ice Cold in Alex* and *Lawrence of Arabia*. Stills by courtesy of ITC.

TOP LEFT: Singing stars turned actors David Essex (l.) and Adam Faith in the musical *Stardust* with Adam Faith giving a convincing portrait of an agent/manager in the tough world of pop adulation and promotion. Directed by Michael Apted for Good Time Enterprises in 1974.

TOP RIGHT: Meet *Tommy*, as played by Roger Daltry in the 1975 Hemdale/Stigwood production, directed by Ken Russell. The Pete Townshend rock opera tells of a deaf, dumb and blind child who becomes a rock idol. Also starring were Eric Clapton, Elton John, Ann-Margret and Oliver Reed.

CENTRE LEFT: Screen mother and daughter (Vanessa Redgrave and Susan George) find their dull wintry seaside resort somewhat brightened with the appearance of an old flame in the shape of Cliff Robertson. *Out of Season* was directed by Alan Bridges and produced for EMI/Lorimar in 1975 by Robert Enders and Merv Adelson.

BOTTOM: Ralph Richardson and Richard Briers were heard but not seen in key voice roles for the £2,000,000 animation film of Richard Adams's best-seller *Watership Down*. Who would have thought that this sad and moral tale about rabbits would have been the surprise success of 1978 that it was? A fact that must have delighted producer Martin Rosen and director John Hubley. Amongst the many familiar voices used were those of Denholm Elliott, Julian Glover, Hannah Gordon, Nigel Hawthorne, Michael Hordern, John Hurt, Roy Kinnear and Zero Mostel.

TOP: Another 1976 success was *Bugsy Malone*, director Alan Parker's feature film debut. A spoof on the 30s gangster period, played tongue-in-cheek by a cast of children, gave the sad British production scene of the 70s a much-needed fillip. Unbelievably adult performances came from Scott Baio, Jodie Foster, John Cassisi, Florrie Dugger and Martin Lev in this Alan Marshall production with David Puttnam as executive producer. The film was yet one more British production to receive part of its financial backing from the National Film Finance Corporation.

CENTRE: Main cast of David Frost and Stuart Lyons's production of the Cinderella story, *The Slipper and the Rose*. (L. to r.) Rosalind Ayres, Sherrie Hewson, Julian Orchard, Kenneth More, Michael Hordern, Christopher Gable, Polly Williams. (Front row) Margaret Lockwood, Edith Evans, Richard Chamberlain, Gemma Craven, Lally Bowers, Annette Crosbie, Stuart Lyons (front left) and Bryan Forbes who directed the film, at Pinewood Studios in 1976.

BOTTOM LEFT: Poster for *The Man who Fell to Earth*, produced by Michael Deeley and Barry Spikings. In 1976, their company British Lion merged with EMI, and they became joint managing directors of EMI Films Ltd. Nicholas Roeg directed David Bowie, Rip Torn, Candy Clark and Buck Henry in this drama of an extra-terrestrial visitor failing in his attempt to colonise the world.

BOTTOM RIGHT: German agents in disguise, Michael Caine and Donald Sutherland greet Jean Marsh on their arrival in an English village during World War II in their attempt to assassinate Winston Churchill. *The Eagle has Landed* was directed in 1976 by John Sturges and produced by Jack Wiener and David Niven Junior.

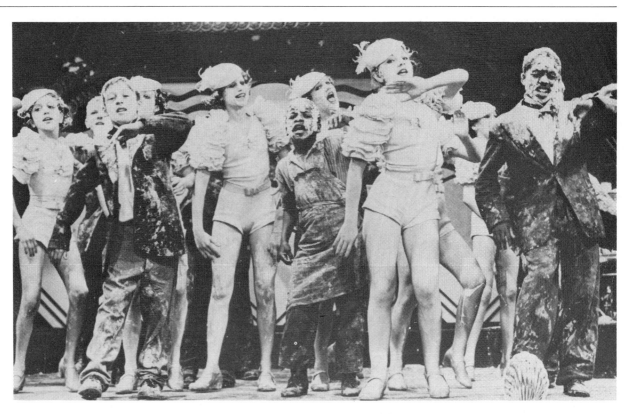

A British Film Collection would not be complete without mention of the second-to-none expertise that produced special effects, sets and gadgetry for some of the blockbusters of the 70s at British studios including Pinewood and Elstree. Pinewood became host studio to the Bond films where the world's largest sound stages and tanks were built for the massive submarine set for *The Spy Who Loved Me* produced for United Artists by Albert Broccoli in 1977 and directed by Lewis Gilbert. Pinewood also shared the honours with Shepperton in teaching *Superman* (Christopher Reeve) to fly, as well as making outstanding exterior sets for this Alexander/Ilya Salkind presentation directed in 1977 by Richard Donner. Pierre Spengler co-produced.

TOP LEFT: The 007 Stage at Pinewood for *The Spy Who Loved Me.* © 1977 Danjaq S.A.

TOP RIGHT: Pinewood studios.

BOTTOM: Christopher Reeve as Superman.

TOP: (L. to r.) Keith Carradine, Harvey Keitel and director Ridley Scott pace out a scene for *The Duellists*, the story of two officers in Napoleon's army who cross swords early in their careers and continue to do so for the next 16 years. Well-plumbed characterisations with an excellent screenplay from Gerald Vaughan-Hughes made this 1977 NFFC/David Puttnam production an entertaining film. Tom Conti, Albert Finney, Edward Fox, Diana Quick and Robert Stephens also appeared.

BOTTOM: Kenneth Maidment, President of the British Film and Television Producers' Association, being presented to HM Queen Elizabeth, the Queen Mother by Cecil Bernstein at the Royal Film Performance of *The Silver Streak* in 1977. Facing the camera is Percy Livingstone, President of the Society of Film Distributors and left of the group, Brian Tessler, Managing Director of London Weekend Television. The present British Film and Television Producers' Association consists of the old British Film Producers' Association (formed in 1941) and the Federation of British Filmmakers (formed in 1957). The BFTPA represents the interests of the production side of the industry. Its membership includes major production companies, studios and British production subsidiaries of American companies. It is an employer association, therefore industrial relations are a vital part of its activities and it is in constant contact with all film unions. It has also joined with the Independent Programme Producers' Association to form a joint relations service. The BFTPA has many committees, including an overseas committee that represents British production abroad at film festivals and markets. Still by courtesy of PIC Photos.

Elstree Studios were also producing their own blend of magic in 1977 in the shape of the blockbuster *Star Wars*. Produced for 20th Century-Fox by Gary Kurtz it was directed by George Lucas. British and American expertise went on to win four Oscars for best sound, visual effects, costume design and art direction. By December 1980 the film had grossed over 500,000,000 dollars world-wide. *The Empire Strikes Back* and *Return of the Jedi* were also made at Elstree studios as well as the USA.

TOP: Darth Vader (David Prowse) in a scene from *The Empire Strikes Back*. Stills by courtesy of 20th Century-Fox.

BOTTOM: Bossy See Threepio (Anthony Daniels) endeavours to direct operations in *Star Wars* while his chubby little friend Artoo Detoo (Kenny Baker) doubtless plans his own strategy.

INSET: Thorn-EMI Elstree Studios.

TOP LEFT: Safely back across the Rhine, Sean Connery has a 'scratchy' meeting with his superior officer, Dirk Bogarde in Joseph Levine's production for United Artists *A Bridge Too Far*, directed by Richard Attenborough in 1977.

TOP RIGHT: David Niven and Angela Lansbury in *Death on the Nile*.

CENTRE LEFT: (L. to r.) David Niven, George Kennedy, Peter Ustinov, Lois Chiles, Simon MacCorkindale, Bette Davis, Jack Warden, Maggie Smith,

Angela Lansbury and commanding their undivided attention, is I. S. Johar in *Death on the Nile* directed in 1978 by John Guillermin. The screenplay of Agatha Christie's novel was by Anthony Shaffer; John Brabourne and Richard Goodwin produced for EMI.

BOTTOM LEFT: Rank Film Distributors is one of Britain's largest independent film distribution companies, offering a wide range of major feature films for theatrical release, video and television. The company was formed in 1935 and moved into the current purpose-built offices at 127 Wardour Street, London in 1936. Still by courtesy of PIC Photos.

BOTTOM RIGHT: Legend has it that when Michael Winner made his directorial debut in 1957 with a travelogue called *This is Belgium*, his budget was so limited that most of the film was shot in East Grinstead. Not so for the 1977 Elliot Kastner/Jerry Bick production for Lew Grade of *The Big Sleep*. Michael Winner directed this film and TV adaptation of Raymond Chandler's novel with a strong cast including Diana Quick. Still by courtesy of ITC.

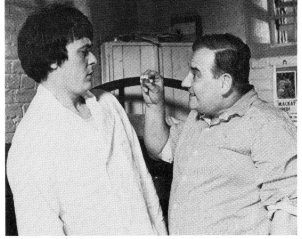

TOP LEFT: **Stevie (1978)**
Poetess Stevie Smith (Glenda
Jackson) watches her fiance
(Alec McCowen) in mindless
banter with her maiden aunt
(Mona Washbourne). Trevor
Howard also starred. Hugh
Whitemore's screenplay was
directed and produced by
Robert Enders, with
photography by Freddie
Young.

TOP RIGHT: The art of
double-talk as demonstrated
here by Ronnie Barker to an
unimpressed Richard
Beckinsale while 'doing time'
in *Porridge*, the Black Lion/
Witzend production for

exhibition and television
release, directed by Dick
Clement in 1979.

CENTRE LEFT: Tom Bell and
Shope Sodeinde in a scene
from *The Sailor's Return*,
about a sailor who brings
home a black bride with
tragic results. Directed by
Jack Gold, it was produced
for Euston Films in 1978 by
Otto Plaschkes.

CENTRE RIGHT: Four men,
four soldiers, four mercen-
aries — the four leaders of
The Wild Geese: (l. to r.)
Richard Harris, Roger
Moore, Richard Burton and
Hardy Kruger in the Euan
Lloyd Production of 1978,
directed by Andrew V.
McLaglen.

BOTTOM: Robert Powell
clings desperately to the
hand of Big Ben in a last-
minute bid to prevent the
timed mechanism setting off
a bomb device. A Greg
Smith-Norfolk International
Production for Rank of *The
Thirty-Nine Steps*, the 1978
remake of the John Buchan
thriller, directed at Pinewood
by Don Sharp.

TOP LEFT: Stage and screen actor Ian Holm came to prominence with the Royal Shakespeare Company at Stratford and the Aldwych Theatre before making his film debut in 1968 in *The Bofors Gun*. Other film appearances followed in *Nicholas and Alexander, Mary Queen of Scots, Young Winston* and (here) *All Quiet on the Western Front*. Produced by Norman Rosemont for ITC and directed in 1979 by Delbert Mann.

TOP RIGHT: Kate (Hazel O'Connor) whose talents and sanity are jeopardised by the machinations of the rock-music power structure, rehearses one of her numbers accompanied by the band (l. to r.) Jonathan Pryce, Gary Tibbs and Mark Wingett in *Breaking Glass*. This Davina Belling/Clive Parsons production was directed in 1979 by Brian Gibson.

CENTRE LEFT: *The Bitch:* Joan Collins in her now famous pose in the role of Fontaine Khaled, a beautiful, high-living pleasure seeking divorcee. The John Quested production was directed for Brent Walker by Gerry O'Hara in 1979. Still courtesy of Brent Walker.

CENTRE RIGHT: Frances de la Tour and Leonard Rossiter in *Rising Damp*. Rossiter brought his hilarious television characterisation of Rigsby, the unpredictable boarding house owner to this big-screen presentation for Black Lion Films. Roy Skeggs produced from a screenplay by Eric Chappell. Joe McGrath directed in 1979. Still by courtesy of ITC.

BOTTOM: *The Elephant Man* (John Hurt), so appallingly deformed that he wears a sack over his head to avoid ridicule, makes his way to visit a Victorian surgeon (Anthony Hopkins) in the hope of treatment for the disease which turns out, sadly, to be incurable. This film, beautifully directed by David Lynch, is based on a true story and won wide acclaim on its release in 1979. Produced for EMI Films by Jonathan Sanger, it also starred Wendy Hiller and John Gielgud.

The British are coming

1980-1984

AND SO the British film industry limped into the 80s, fragmented and frustrated.

In 1979 Thorn, the British electrical giant, took over EMI and with the amalgamation, the studios changed their name to Thorn-EMI Elstree Studios. They and Rank's Pinewood were still the largest studios in the country, followed by Bray, Bushey, Halliford, Isleworth, Shepperton, St. John's Wood, Twickenham and Wembley, the leading British cinema circuit exhibitors in the early 80s being Brent Walker, Caledonian, Cannon, Granada, Rank, Star and Thorn-EMI, with Rank and Thorn-EMI as the dominant houses.

Although the decade had a slow start, a delightful low-budget 1980 feature, *Gregory's Girl*, produced by Davina Belling and Clive Parsons and directed by Bill Forsyth, received an excellent reception while *The Long Good Friday*, with Bob Hoskins and Helen Mirren, also turned out to be a surprise success.

The following year, David Puttnam with courage, dedication and against increasing odds, produced *Chariots of Fire*, which was directed by Hugh Hudson. It claimed four Oscars including the award for best picture. 'The British are coming,' declared Colin Welland who had just received his Oscar for the film's screenplay — and he was right. *Chariots of Fire* was to mark the resurgence of the British film industry. That is not to say that the film companies and investment trusts changed their attitudes overnight and queued to finance British productions — nor, incredible as it may sound, David Puttnam's next feature. But the point had at least been brought home to them, that excellent British films could be made on modest budgets. No small measure of credit must also go to Goldcrest Films for helping in no uncertain terms, to put the industry back on its feet. Founded in 1977, the company provided development funding for *Chariots of Fire* and *Local Hero*, and developed a positive partnership policy towards independent British producers, American majors, Channel 4 and the National Film Finance Corporation. Continuing to back a number of major British films, Goldcrest also quickly moved into sales and distribution as well as mounting its own production programme.

Hard on the heels of *Chariots of Fire* came *Gandhi*, a film that producer/director Richard Attenborough had waited nearly 20 years to make. It swept the board in 1983 by winning eight Oscars, including best film, best director and best actor award for its star Ben Kingsley. The British film industry was back in business with a vengeance.

1983 also marked the return to the screen of not one, but two James Bonds, with debonair Roger Moore surrounded by nuclear devices and lovely Maud Adams in *Octopussy* which was made at Pinewood; and rugged Sean Connery steeped in special stunt wizardry and beautiful women in *Never Say Never Again*, made at the Elstree Studios. In 1982 *The Draughtsman's Contract* had become an artistic and commercial success for the BFI, who celebrated their 50th Anniversary in 1983. *The French Lieutenant's Woman, Local Hero, Educating Rita* and *Heat and Dust* were all outstanding box-office successes.

Understandably, a new feeling of optimism and enthusiasm surrounded the industry — that is just up to the spring budget of 1984. In this, the Chancellor announced, along with other measures, the effective demise after April 1985 of capital allowances, which in turn affected essential film investment. A major setback to an industry that has only just begun the long haul back into international film markets — which no doubt will be rectified in the future. The abolition of the Eady Levy and the privatisation of the NFFC also appears likely.

As this book goes to press at the beginning of April 1984, a number of British films have either just been completed or are still in production. There will be some amongst them that will undoubtedly stand as some of the finest ever to have emerged from the United Kingdom. *The Dresser* and *Educating Rita* received Oscar nominations; *Greystoke: The Legend of Tarzan, Lord of the Apes*, in which Ralph Richardson gave his last film performance and to whom the film is dedicated, is due for international release; David Lean is busy directing the John Brabourne/Richard Goodwin production of *A Passage to India; Yentl* is about to have its world première; Goldcrest and the NFFC are producing *Another Country*, while *The Shooting Party* and *Secret Places* are well into schedule.

A fitting and proud comment on which to end this tribute to the British film industry.

TOP LEFT:
Gregory's Girl (1980)
The goal Dee Hepburn has in mind is the vacancy on the football team while Gordon John Sinclair has his heart set on a sporting activity of a different nature. A delightful, warm-hearted film, written and directed by Bill Forsyth. Davina Belling and Clive Parsons produced this low budget, box-office success.

TOP RIGHT: Popular television comedy couple *George and Mildred* (Yootha Joyce and Brian Murphy) came to the big screen in 1980 in the Roy Skeggs production, directed by Peter Frazer-Jones.

CENTRE: Bob Hoskins and Helen Mirren starred in *The Long Good Friday*, set in the East End of London involving a crook planning a property deal with the help of the IRA Mafia. Rival factions from the underworld have other plans and a bloody gang-war ensues, brutally ending his aspirations for a gambling leisure complex. Produced by Barry Hanson in 1980 it was expertly directed by John MacKenzie.

BOTTOM: David Essex and Cristina Raines with the *Silver Dream Racer*, a story of a young man obsessed with motor-cycle racing, preferring to play roulette with his life than settling down to the domesticated life sought by his girl-friend. Written and directed by David Wickes, produced by Rene Dupont in 1980.

TOP: The 'Nostromo' search party discuss the remains of a non-human pilot — the space jockey in *Alien*. The splendid visual effects were to win an Oscar for their creators, Brian Johnson, Nick Allder, Denys Ayling and H. R. Giger in director Ridley Scott's 1980 nerve-tingling space thriller, produced by Walter Hill, Gordon Carroll and David Giler. Appearing in the film were Sigourney Weaver, John Hurt, Ian Holm and Tom Skerritt.

INSET: Oscar-winning *Chariots of Fire*. Hailed as a triumph worldwide, this film was to mark the resurgence of the British Film Industry, to which no small measure of credit must go to its producer, David Puttnam, whose courage and dedication against increasing odds, ensured that the film would be made. An Enigma Production for 20th Century-Fox, it was directed by Hugh Hudson from a screenplay by Colin Welland in 1981. On location, Hugh Hudson (l.) and David Puttnam.

BOTTOM: The 1924 Olympic Games, and Eric Liddell (Ian Charleson) wins for Great Britain to the joy of other members of the team: (r. to l.) Ben Cross who played Harold Abrahams, Nicholas Farrell, Daniel Gerroll and Nigel Havers.

TOP LEFT: Meryl Streep and Jeremy Irons in *The French Lieutenant's Woman*, another great success of 1981, directed by Karel Reisz and produced by Leon Clore for United Artists. Harold Pinter's screenplay of John Fowles's novel had a twin-layered narrative: a Victorian infatuation and a modern-day affair with Jeremy Irons and Meryl Streep playing both couples. The film's production was based at Twickenham studios.

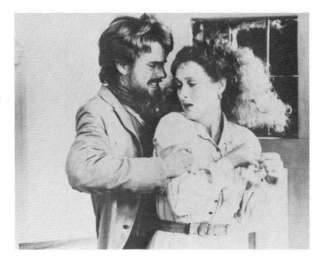

TOP RIGHT: More magic and wizardry produced by Jim Henson and Gary Kurtz at the Elstree studios for *The Dark Crystal*, an adventure fantasy set in another world and another time. Directed for ITC Films International by Jim Henson and Frank Oz in 1981.

CENTRE: Richard Attenborough and Ben Kingsley share a brief moment of relaxation during the filming of *Gandhi* (1982). Following the success of *Chariots of Fire*, came *Gandhi*, a prestigious, eight-Oscars winner that director/producer Richard Attenborough had waited 20 years to make. The life of Mohandas K. Gandhi manifested itself not only from the epic production, but also through the remarkable performance of Ben Kingsley in the leading role. A strong supporting cast included Candice Bergen, Edward Fox, John Gielgud, Geraldine James, John Mills and many others. Shepperton Studios were the home base for the production.

BOTTOM LEFT: *Friend or Foe*. Breakfast time and the first morning as Jerry (John Bardon) the farmer and his wife Anne (Stacy Tendetter) try to get to know something about the two evacuee boys (Mark Luxford and John Holmes) who have come to live with them. A scene from the award-winning Children's Film Foundation production of 1982 which was produced by Gordon L.T. Scott and directed by John Krish.

BOTTOM RIGHT: Maggie Smith and Peter Ustinov in *Evil Under the Sun*. Agatha Christie's super sleuth, Hercule Poirot is at it again in this 1982 John Brabourne/ Richard Goodwin production directed by Guy Hamilton.

TOP LEFT: Publicity still of Julie Andrews in *Victor/Victoria*, produced by Blake Edwards and Tony Adams and also directed by Blake Edwards in 1982. A former child singing artist she rose to stardom in such stage shows as *The Boy Friend* and then with the smash-hit *My Fair Lady*. International success followed with films including *The Sound of Music*, *Mary Poppins*, *Thoroughly Modern Millie*, *Star* and *Darling Lili*.

TOP RIGHT: Margaret (Glenda Jackson) and Chris (Alan Bates), who had an idyllic love affair in their youth, are reunited 15 years later. A scene from the Brent Walker/Barry R. Cooper/Screba Film production of *The Return of the Soldier*, which was directed by Alan Bridges from Hugh Whitemore's screenplay. Also starring were Ann-Margret and Julie Christie. The film was produced by Anne Skinner and Simon Relph and released in 1982.

CENTRE RIGHT: Leonard Rossiter fearfully accepts the fact that all might not be ready after all for the expected Royal visit to *Britannia Hospital* — a hard-hitting satire directed by Lindsay Anderson and produced by Davina Belling and Clive Parsons in 1982.

BOTTOM: The big man (Dan Meaden) finds himself cornered by James Bond (Sean Connery) in *Never Say Never Again*. Connery returned to the role after an absence of some years to a warm welcome. Producer Jack Schwartzman and director Irvin Kershner ensured that pace, glamour, beautiful girls and out-standing stunts surrounded their 1983 Fleming hero both in the Bahamas and Elstree Studios.

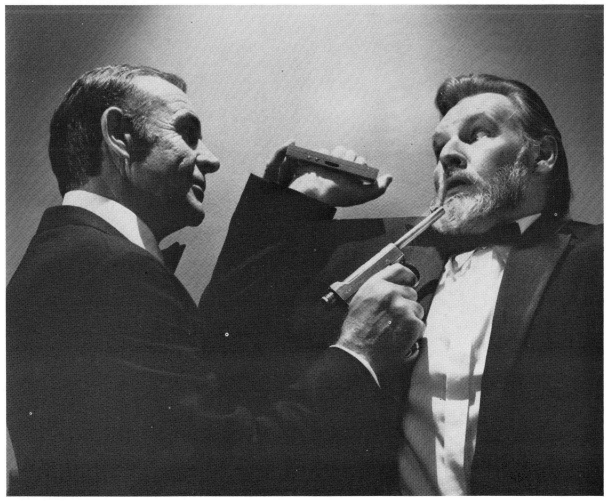

TOP LEFT: **The Draughtsman's Contract (1982)** An artistic, commercial success for the British Film Institute which produced this period mystery. It was directed by Peter Greenaway in conjunction with Channel 4 Television, and starred (centre group) Janet Suzman (r.), Anthony Higgins and Anne Louise Lambert.

TOP RIGHT: Lewis Gilbert (l.), Julie Walters and Michael Caine on the set of *Educating Rita* (1983). Willy Russell's play, from which he wrote the scenario, was originally commissioned by the Royal Shakespeare Company and ran successfully at London's Piccadilly Theatre for more than two years. The story of a blunt young hairdresser seeking academic enlightenment from a disillusioned, alcoholic professor had a great deal of touching humour and pathos. It was beautifully produced and directed by Lewis Gilbert.

LONG PICTURE: The villagers of the Scottish coastal village of Ferness await the arrival of the American oil mogul whose decision, whether or not to construct an oil refining plant in the region, will alter the course of all their lives. A scene from *Local Hero* directed from his own screenplay by Bill Forsyth and produced by David Puttnam in 1983. Leading players were Burt Lancaster, Denis Lawson, Fulton Mackay and Peter Reigert.

THIRD LEFT: Captain Terri Daniels (Denis Quilley) and his gay ensemble, Corporal Len Bonny (Joe Melia) and Sergeant Eric Young-Love (Simon Jones) do their 'Carmen Miranda' number for the troops in *Privates on Parade*.

THIRD RIGHT: Continuing the family tradition, producer Simon Relph (centre) discusses manoeuvres with director Michael Blakemore (r.) and John Cleese while filming *Privates on Parade*, released in 1983.

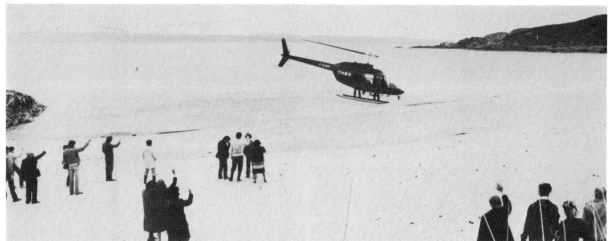

658-26a

ROGER MOORE with the "OCTOPUSSY" girls in the latest James Bond film Produced by Albert R. Broccoli and directed by John Glen. Distributed by United International Pictures (UK).

OPPOSITE, BOTTOM: The Bishop (Denholm Elliott) pays *The Missionary* (Michael Palin) a visit to warn him that his religious rivals are jealous and may expose his unorthodox methods of recruiting 'fallen' women. A scene from the Handmade Films presentation, written by Michael Palin. This Michael Palin/ Neville C. Thompson production of 1983 is 'a tragicomic comedy set at the heyday of the British Empire' and directed by Richard Loncraine. Also starring were Graham Crowden, Michael Hordern, Trevor Howard and Phoebe Nicholls. Photograph by David Farrell.

MAIN PICTURE: **Octopussy** Roger Moore also returned in 1983 to the role of Commander James Bond 007. Special stunt wizardry, a delicious Maud Adams, mysterious Louis Jourdan, nuclear devices and a priceless Fabergé egg, all added up to marvellous screen entertainment.

BELOW: Publicity still for *Slayground*, the EMI crime thriller based on Richard Stark's novel, produced in 1983 by John Dark and Gower Frost. Directed by Terry Bedford, it starred Peter Coyote, Mel Smith and Billie Whitelaw.

TOP: HRH The Princess Anne, Mrs. Mark Phillips, President of the British Academy of Film and Television Arts, presenting Sir Richard Attenborough CBE, the Academy's Vice President, with a Fellowship — BAFTA's highest accolade — at the 1982 Awards ceremony (20th March, 1983). Timothy Burrill, the then Chairman of the Academy, looks on. The objects of the British Academy of Film and Television Arts are to promote, maintain, improve and advance original and creative work among persons engaged in film and television production; to create and maintain a high standard of qualification and performance in such persons; and to encourage and promote experiment and research in the arts, sciences and techniques of film and television production. The Academy acts as a forum for ideas which are expressed through meetings and seminars held regularly at BAFTA, advises Government Departments in Britain and other countries on matters concerning Film and Television and through its Awards upholds standards within the industry. The Academy has close ties with similar Academies overseas.

BOTTOM: **The British Film Institute, 1933-1983**
HRH The Prince of Wales, presenting the BFI's Chairman, Sir Richard Attenborough, with the Royal Charter to mark the Institute's 50th anniversary. The ceremony took place at the Guildhall in October 1983. Colonel John Buchan, distinguished soldier, Member of Parliament and writer — the Institute's first Governor — would surely have viewed with understandable pride, the BFI's success over the decades. The BFI, which incorporates the National Film Archive, the National Film Theatre and their production and information divisions has as its slogan 'To encourage the Arts of Film and Television.' This might appear a little modest in the light of its achievements, but Sir Richard Attenborough was to put the situation into perspective in his anniversary speech when he said 'The important thing about the Institute is that it is the only organisation which historically and academically reflects the achievement of film as a contributory art form to the heritage of this country.' Still by courtesy of the BFI Stills Library.

TOP : Banqueting scene at the Nawab's Palace from *Heat and Dust* (1983) produced by Ismail Merchant and directed by James Ivory. Written by Ruth Prawer Jhabvala this film marked the 21st anniversary of Merchant/Ivory, whose productions include *The Europeans* and *Quartet.*

CENTRE: *Monty Python's the Meaning of Life*, produced by John Goldstone and directed by Terry Jones in 1983.

BOTTOM LEFT: *The Plough-man's Lunch* for Jonathan Pryce in Simon Relph's production of 1983, directed by Richard Eyre. The film pinpointed the very real problems faced by journalists and researchers in today's jet-paced communications world, in which they occasionally have to choose between their moral values and the media's appetite for instant news. The film was a winner, partly due to its topicality and also for accurately reflecting today's world of double standards.

BOTTOM RIGHT: *Dragonslayer.* A Paramount Picture in association with Walt Disney Productions. Produced by Hal Barwood and directed by Matthew Robins in 1983. Peter MacNicol is seen here with Sir Ralph Richardson.

MONTY PYTHON'S THE MEANING OF LIFE

The Pythons (L-R: TERRY JONES, JOHN CLEESE, TERRY GILLIAM, GRAHAM CHAPMAN, ERIC IDLE, MICHAEL PALIN) meet on the battlefield of Rorke's Drift in the Boer War.

DRAGONSLAYER

TOP: As this book goes to press, early in 1984 a number of British films have either just been completed or are still in production. Among them will be some that will undoubtedly emerge as some of the finest we have ever produced. *The Dresser*, starring Albert Finney (l.) and Tom Courtenay, produced and directed by Peter Yates, has already received five Oscar nominations, including best actor, best picture and best director.

BOTTOM LEFT: *Secret Places* stars (l. to r.) Marie-Therese Relin, Jenny Agutter and Tara MacGowran. Produced by Skreba/Virgin in association with the National Film Finance Corporation. Produced by Simon Relph and Ann Skinner and directed in 1984 by Zelda Barron.

BOTTOM RIGHT:
A Passage to India
Directed by David Lean, seen here on location with Peggy Ashcroft. A John Brabourne/Richard Goodwin production in 1984, with a screenplay adapted from E. M. Forster's novel by David Lean. The all-star cast includes Victor Bannerjee, Judy Davis, James Fox, Alec Guinness, Nigel Havers.

OPPOSITE MARGIN: *Another Country*. A 1984 Goldcrest presentation in association with the National Film Finance Corporation, produced by Alan Marshall and directed by Marek Kanievska. Established in 1977, Goldcrest quickly moved from providing initial funding finance to production, sales and distribution. Goldcrest's positive partnership policy towards The National Film Finance Corporation, Channel 4 and American Majors as well as consolidating their associations with established producers like Richard Attenborough and David Puttnam — has resulted in a major British film company. Rupert Everett (l.) and Colin Firth are two of the actors in this film version of Julian Mitchell's play set in a public school. The film highlights the educational, social and sexual problems encountered by the inmates which subsequently guides them towards their eventual political persuasions.

TOP: *The Shooting Party*, produced from the novel by Isabel Colegate by Geoffrey Reeve and directed by Alan Bridges, will be released in the autumn of 1984. (L. to r.) Edward Fox, Aharon Ipalé, James Mason, Dorothy Tutin, Joris Stuyk, Judi Bowker, Rupert Frazer, Warren Saire (in front) Robert Hardy, Rebecca Saire, Cheryl Campbell, Sarah Badel.

Greystoke: The Legend of Tarzan, Lord of the Apes (1984)
A Hugh Hudson film starring Ralph Richardson, Ian Holm, James Fox and introducing Christopher Lambert, Andie MacDowell, produced by Hugh Hudson and Stanley S. Canter, screenplay by P. H. Vazak and Michael Austin. Based on the story *Tarzan of the Apes* by Edgar Rice Burroughs. Directed by Hugh Hudson.

CENTRE: In 1886, following a shipwreck off the West Coast of Africa, an infant child became part of a family of apes who raised and protected him. As he grew up, he learned the laws of the jungle and eventually claimed the title, Lord of the Apes.

BOTTOM: Years later, the Lord of the Apes returns to civilisation, but remains uncertain as to which laws he should obey . . . those of man or those of the jungle.

IT IS FITTING that this book should end with a look to the future. Barker, Hepworth, Acres, and their contemporaries started the British Film industry rolling into the 20th Century nearly 90 years ago. What better image could there be, than the young film makers of today continuing into the 21st century with these students from the National Film and Television School filming *Cuban Breeze,* directed by Colin Villa, 1984. Still by courtesy of Richard Coward.

The National Film School began its three year programme of instruction in the autumn of 1971 at the Beaconsfield Film Studios with an initial intake of 25 students. Among those first students were Bill Forsyth (*Gregory's Girl; Local Hero*), and Michael Radford (*Another Time, Another Place; 1984*). Other graduates now occupy leading positions in the film and television industry (including Maggie Brooks who wrote the script of *Loose Connections* and Jim O'Brien, co-director of *The Jewel in the Crown*) as animators, cameramen/women, directors, editors, executives and producers. The first graduate of the NFTS to win an Oscar was Lloyd Phillips (producer) for *Dollar Bottom* which was directed and scored by fellow graduates Roger Christian and Trevor Jones. The first school film to win a British Academy Award was David Anderson's *Dreamland Express* — best animation film (1982). In 1982 the name of the School was changed to the National Film and Television School in recognition of its growing responsibility for training in all aspects of television production. Also in 1982 the School launched a pilot scheme for re-training which led to the establishment of the National Short Course Training Programme which operates as a separate unit at the School's premises in Beaconsfield. The Director, Colin Young, received the Michael Balcon award from the British Academy in 1984.

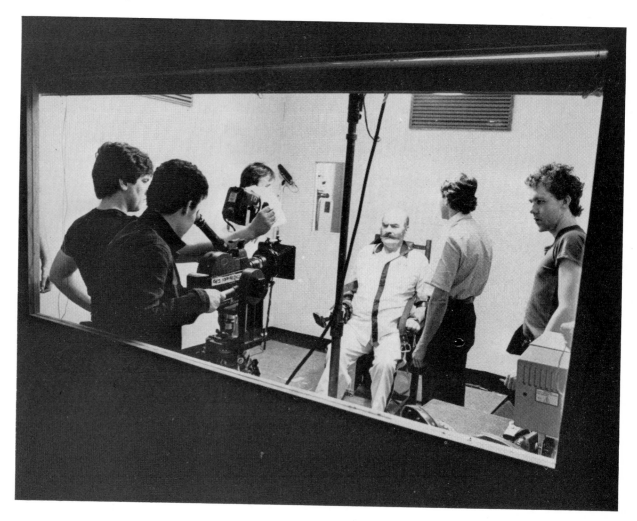

Bibliography

The Bioscope

The British Film and Television Year Book 1946-1983 Peter Noble (Screen International Publications)

The British Film Catalogue 1895-1970 Denis Gifford (David & Charles, 1973)

The British Film Industry, PEP Reports (Political & Economic Planning, 1952)

The British Film Industry Yearbook 1948 (Film Press Ltd)

British Films Cannes Brochures

British Films 1971-1981 (British Film Institute 1983)

Cinema in Britain Ivan Butler (A. S. Barnes/Tantivy Press 1973)

Comedy Films 1894-1954 John Montgomery (Allen & Unwin, 1968)

The Contemporary Cinema Penelope Houston (Penguin Books 1963)

A Critical History of British Cinema R. Armes (Secker & Warburg, 1978)

Ealing Studios Charles Barr (Cameron Tayleur/David & Charles 1977)

Elstree: The British Hollywood Patricia Warren (Elm Tree Books, 1983)

The Film Business Ernest Betts (Allen & Unwin, 1973)

Film Guide, 4th Edition Leslie Halliwell (Granada, 1983)

Film Weekly 1928-1929 (English Newspapers Ltd)

Filmgoer's Companion, 6th Edition Leslie Halliwell (Granada, 1972)

Flashback: An Autobiography of a British Film-maker George Pearson (Allen & Unwin, 1957)

Good Morning Boys: Will Hay Roy Seaton and Ray Martin (Barrie & Jenkins, 1978)

The Great British Picture Show George Perry (Paladin, 1975)

The Guinness Book of Film Facts and Figures Patrick Robertson (Guinness Superlatives Ltd, 1980)

History of the British Film Rachel Low (4 vols, Allen & Unwin, 1973)

The International Encyclopedia of Film Edited by R. Manwell (Michael Joseph, 1972)

International Film Encyclopedia Ephraim Katz (Macmillan, 1980)

Kinematograph Weekly and *Kine Weekly 1920-1971* (Odhams Press)

Kinematograph Year Books, 1914-1970 (Odhams Press)

A Lifetime of Films Michael Balcon (Hutchinson, 1969)

Michael Balcon's 25 Years in Films Edited by M. Danischewsky (World Film Publications, 1947)

Miracle of the Movies Leslie Wood (Burke Publishing Company, 1947)

Nice Work, Adrian Brunel Forbes Robertson (1949)

Oxford Companion to Film (Oxford University Press, 1976)

Penguin Film Review (Penguin Books, 1946)

Picturegoer (Odhams Press)

Picture Show Annual, 1926/1932 (Odhams Press)

The Pleasure Dome Graham Greene (Secker & Warburg, 1972)

Screen & TV International, 1971 — current 1984 Edited by Peter Noble (King Publications Ltd)

A Short History of the Movies Gerald Mast (Bobbs-Merrill Company Inc., 1976)

Twenty-Five Thousand Sunsets Herbert Wilcox (The Bodley Head, 1967)

World Encyclopedia of Film Cawkwell & Smith (Studio Vista, 1972)

World Film Encyclopedia Edited by C. Winchester (Amalgamated Press, 1933)

Index of films

Producers, directors and stars of all films illustrated are given in the stills captions.

Index